T0302556

Acquiring Publicly Available Information Analytic Tools in a Proprietary Marketplace

Acquisition Recommendations for Army Cyber Command

WILLIAM MARCELLINO, MICHAEL SCHWILLE, KRISTIN WARREN, CHRISTOPHER PAUL, EDDIE LÓPEZ III, JAMES RYSEFF

Prepared for the United States Army
Approved for public release; distribution is unlimited.

RAND ARROYO CENTER

For more information on this publication, visit **www.rand.org/t/RRA2500-1**.

About RAND

The RAND Corporation is a research organization that develops solutions to public policy challenges to help make communities throughout the world safer and more secure, healthier and more prosperous. RAND is nonprofit, nonpartisan, and committed to the public interest. To learn more about RAND, visit www.rand.org.

Research Integrity

Our mission to help improve policy and decisionmaking through research and analysis is enabled through our core values of quality and objectivity and our unwavering commitment to the highest level of integrity and ethical behavior. To help ensure our research and analysis are rigorous, objective, and nonpartisan, we subject our research publications to a robust and exacting quality-assurance process; avoid both the appearance and reality of financial and other conflicts of interest through staff training, project screening, and a policy of mandatory disclosure; and pursue transparency in our research engagements through our commitment to the open publication of our research findings and recommendations, disclosure of the source of funding of published research, and policies to ensure intellectual independence. For more information, visit www.rand.org/about/research-integrity.

RAND's publications do not necessarily reflect the opinions of its research clients and sponsors.

Published by the RAND Corporation, Santa Monica, Calif.
© 2024 RAND Corporation
RAND® is a registered trademark.

Library of Congress Cataloging-in-Publication Data is available for this publication.
ISBN: 978-1-9774-1211-9

Cover: Zoonar GmbH/Alamy.

Limited Print and Electronic Distribution Rights

This publication and trademark(s) contained herein are protected by law. This representation of RAND intellectual property is provided for noncommercial use only. Unauthorized posting of this publication online is prohibited; linking directly to its webpage on rand.org is encouraged. Permission is required from RAND to reproduce, or reuse in another form, any of its research products for commercial purposes. For information on reprint and reuse permissions, please visit www.rand.org/pubs/permissions.

About This Report

This report documents research and analysis conducted as part of a project entitled *Artificial Intelligence and Machine Learning for Social Media in an Environment of Proprietary Capabilities*, sponsored by U.S. Army Cyber Command (ARCYBER). The purpose of the project was to inform ARCYBER on how to effectively acquire and develop social media data analytics capabilities—to include data, analysis methods and tools, and related platforms—leveraging both commercial solutions and in-house data science and development, security, and information technology operations capabilities.

This research was conducted within RAND Arroyo Center's Forces and Logistics Program. RAND Arroyo Center, part of the RAND Corporation, is a federally funded research and development center (FFRDC) sponsored by the United States Army.

RAND operates under a "Federal-Wide Assurance" (FWA00003425) and complies with the *Code of Federal Regulations for the Protection of Human Subjects Under United States Law* (45 CFR 46), also known as "the Common Rule," as well as with the implementation guidance set forth in DoD Instruction 3216.02. As applicable, this compliance includes reviews and approvals by RAND's Institutional Review Board (the Human Subjects Protection Committee) and by the U.S. Army. The views of sources utilized in this study are solely their own and do not represent the official policy or position of DoD or the U.S. Government.

Acknowledgments

The RAND team gratefully acknowledges LTC David Beskow for his support and insight during this project. We would like to express our gratitude to several people in our sponsoring office, ARCYBER, without whose support this report would not have been possible, including Steven Rehn and COL Marv King. As part of the review process, Eric Wallace and Todd Helmus offered incredibly thoughtful and helpful feedback that significantly improved the report. We received valuable contributions and ideas from personnel across industry, academia, and DoD, so if you have helped us better understand the challenges of publicly available information analytics and how they support DoD and Army missions, thank you. We owe a debt of gratitude to Lauren Skrabala for her creative and editorial support.

Contents

APPENDIXES

Figures and Tables

Figures

Tables

CHAPTER 1

Publicly Available Information Analytic Tools Acquisition for the Army

Publicly available information (PAI) is a critical form of information for use in military operations. As it grows in importance, it is important for the Army to know specifically what PAI is. Department of Defense Directive (DoDD) 3115.18, *DoD Access to and Use of Publicly Available Information (PAI)*, describes PAI as

> information that has been published or broadcast for public consumption, is available on request to the public, is accessible online or otherwise to the public, is available to the public by subscription or purchase, could be seen or heard by a casual observer, is made available at a meeting open to the public, or is obtained by visiting a place or attending an event that is open to the public.[1]

In simple terms, PAI is information that has been published or broadcasted in some manner to the general public and is openly accessible. PAI covers many types of data, including social media (SM) and web data, commercial satellite imagery, census and other government data, various media publications, and technical and gray literature—essentially anything that the public can access freely or by purchase.[2]

DoDD 3115.18 provides direction on PAI and how it can be used within the military. The directive states that DoD personnel are allowed to "access, obtain, and use PAI to plan, inform, enable, execute, and support the full spectrum of DoD missions."[3] However, the Army currently lacks a coordinated system for collecting and analyzing PAI.

Multiple agencies within the Army collect and analyze PAI to support a variety of activities and operations, but these efforts are disconnected and do not leverage economies of

---

[1] DoDD 3115.18, *DoD Access to and Use of Publicly Available Information (PAI)*, June 11, 2019, incorporating change 1, August 20, 2020, pp. 12–13.

[2] The *DoD Dictionary of Military and Associated Terms* does not officially define *PAI*. However, it does define *open-source information* as "[i]nformation that any member of the public could lawfully obtain by request or observation as well as other unclassified information that has limited public distribution or access" (U.S. Department of Defense [DoD], *DoD Dictionary of Military and Associated Terms*, November 2021, p. 159).

[3] DoDD 3115.18, 2020, p. 3.

scale. Multiple data feeds, tools, and solutions are acquired across various units within the Army on an ad hoc basis, without a single proponent or program of record. Army public affairs (PA), civil affairs (CA), psychological operations (PSYOPS), military intelligence, and information advantage organizations all rely on PAI to provide insight and understanding to Army operations and activities.[4] As a result, the Army pays for the same PAI data streams multiple times rather than using a more-efficient and more-cost-effective single enterprise account and shared pool of data. Multiple commands, directorates, and units across echelons need specific data and analytics capabilities and do not know whether these capabilities are already available in other parts of the Army. Efficiently and cost-effectively acquiring PAI capabilities (i.e., data sources and tools), conducting analysis, and providing relevant outputs to multiple elements across the Army (and DoD) requires a coherent approach that leverages economies of scale.[5]

Focus of This Research

The goal of this study is to inform U.S. Army Cyber Command (ARCYBER) efforts to acquire and develop PAI analytic methods, tools, and platforms and to improve the Army's return on investment (ROI) on PAI-enabled efforts. To support this goal, RAND Arroyo Center researchers conducted an inventory of ARCYBER's PAI capability needs; identified available commercial off-the-shelf (COTS) and government off-the-shelf (GOTS) solutions; assessed whether there are gaps in capability coverage; and made recommendations to improve capability investments and support improved collaboration.

Approach

We used multiple methods to carry out this analysis, as described below.

Subject-Matter Expert Interviews

All aspects of this research were informed by 55 interviews that we conducted with subject-matter experts (SMEs) representing a range of academic, industry, interagency, and military perspectives in the PAI space. These included 19 interviews with SMEs within DoD: experts who serve a variety of informational functions across the Army and U.S. Marine Corps, acquisitions experts in the U.S. Navy and Army, experts who work on such joint activ-

---

4 Brian Cheng, Scott Fisher, and Jason C. Morgan, "Find It, Vet It, Share It: The U.S. Government's Open-Source Intelligence Problem and How to Fix It," Modern War Institute at West Point, March 24, 2023; ATP 3-13.1, *The Conduct of Information Operations*, Department of the Army, October 2018.

5 Maggie Smith and Nick Starck, "Open-Source Data Is Everywhere—Except the Army's Concept of Information Advantage," Modern War Institute at West Point, May 24, 2022.

ities as the Joint Military Information Support Operations (MISO) WebOps Center (JMWC) and Joint Information Operations Warfare Center (JIOWC), and experts from the Defense Advanced Research Projects Agency (DARPA). We also conducted 25 interviews with industry SMEs, who represented large DoD prime contractors and startups that provide data and analytic solutions, as well as venture capital firms that advise tech startups interested in DoD clients. We also conducted 11 interviews with academics in consulting groups, technology, and financing who deal with PAI capabilities.

The SME interviews spanned multiple focus areas, including understanding existing COTS/GOTS PAI capabilities and Army needs for those capabilities; identifying of potential barriers to and enablers of the efficient, flexible acquisition of PAI capabilities; and recommending areas for improvement. The interviews were semi-structured and lasted approximately one hour. Both individual and group interviews were held at the unclassified level through Microsoft Teams, a business communication platform. Interview protocols are provided in Appendix A.

PAI Capability Collection and Categorization

Drawing on the interviews described above, we identified Army-relevant existing COTS/GOTS PAI capabilities, excluding piloted-but-not-operationalized demonstrations from the academic and research world. We also collected PAI *tools and reports*—that is, the technical means necessary for those capabilities—using existing tools inventories, open-web searches, and input from SMEs. This resulted in a preliminary inventory of 314 PAI tools and technologies relevant to the Army's PAI needs.[6] We then cleaned and refined the initial list, resulting in a list of 259 tools and technologies.

Scenario-Based Workshops

We conducted a series of scenario-based capabilities analyses to further elicit potential requirements for a robust, relevant PAI analytic capability across the Army. These scenarios were short vignettes covering different situations in which PAI and various capability areas (e.g., PA, law enforcement, operations security, open-source intelligence, military deception, CA, and MISO) could be utilized. The five scenarios that we explored were (1) viral Army stories, (2) force protection, (3) early warning, (4) stability operations, and (5) regime change. Workshop participants included a range of RAND SMEs, such as data scientists, information scientists, experts in operations within the information environment, and CA and PSYOPS practitioners. The scenarios were used to elicit PAI needs by providing contextualized illustrative examples (the scenario protocols are included in Appendix D). We walked through the scenario and discussed the types of data, analytic processes, and tools and capabilities that

[6] The starting point came from the Global Engagement Center's tool list and the Partnership for Analytic Research and Development in the Information Environment (PARDIE)'s tools and capabilities list, as well as additional sources that the RAND team has been asked not to publicly disclose.

would be needed in the scenario, and then identified an Army military occupational specialty or functional area that could potentially be responsible. We used findings from these analyses to identify Army requirements for PAI.

Identification and Categorization of PAI Needs

To identify Army PAI needs, we drew from our SME interviews, surveyed existing DoD operations in the information environment (OIE) capabilities lists, and drew from the scenario-based capabilities workshops.

We created a framework to better understand how PAI analytics sync with military planning processes and operations. Through multiple iterations, we identified four overarching categories of Army capability area requirements for PAI—sense, understand, plan, and assess—each with multiple subcategories. We also identified nine multifunctional capability areas that are used across the four overarching categories for PAI analysis. This framework will be described in more detail in Chapter 2.

We adapted our framework from one created by the 2020 PARDIE OIE Technology Development Roadmap. The PARDIE framework contained approximately 20 headings or categories and roughly 70 required capability areas at varying levels of abstraction.[7] We expanded on this initial framework using other relevant reports and documents across DoD, based on the capabilities each tool was expected to accomplish.[8] We then added to the framework by supplementing capabilities or tasks mentioned in the SME interviews and those identified in the scenario-based capabilities analyses (described below). This produced a framework of tools and capabilities that reached a maximum of 425 tasks and categories, many of which were duplicative or redundant, mismatched in terms of level of abstraction, or were out of the scope of this project. We organized a three-level taxonomy of categories, subcategories, and discrete tasks.

We then refined the task list, removing redundancies, consolidating elements that were part of a discrete task, excluding out-of-scope tasks,[9] and revising or renaming categories to be more descriptive. Tasks that were out of scope include assessment of or recommendations on specific tools or platforms. This consolidation and refinement was conducted over multiple workshops with the full research team, drawing on our expertise as data scientists, military practitioners in information operations, and SMEs in PAI analytics. This resulted in the categorized taxonomy of requirements with five main categories, 19 subcategories,[10] and 172 discrete tasks. The full taxonomy, including discrete tasks, appears in Appendix B.

---

[7] Benjamin Greer and Eric Wallace, "PARDIE OIE Technology Development Roadmap," Joint Information Operations Warfare Center, June 17, 2020.

[8] It was beyond the scope of our project to field test the 314 COTS/GOTS tools in our analysis.

[9] For example, actual conduct of operations in the information environment.

[10] We included a 20th subcategory, "refinement," as part of our PAI process concept as a needed response to planning and assessing efforts. However, because there are no refinement-specific tasks, our PAI tool inventory and gap analysis includes only 19 subcategories.

Crosswalk of Capabilities and Needs

We conducted a crosswalk of the analytic requirements against our inventory of COTS/GOTS solutions (i.e., capabilities). We decomposed the capabilities of the 314 PAI tools in our inventory by matching them against the 19 subcategories of PAI requirements. This allowed us to measure the relative level of coverage across the range of PAI activities (e.g., the number of tools that include visualization, biometrics, geographic information systems [GIS], or assessment capabilities), which is a potential signal for increased investment and development.

We also conducted a crosswalk the subcategory needs we identified against several information capabilities: PA, PSYOPS, CA, military deception, operations security, open-source research, and law enforcement. Each subcategory was ranked using a Likert-like scale and then aggregated across information-related capabilities (IRCs). This allowed us to identify subcategories that have the widest applicability across the Army, another potential signal for increased investment and development.

Identification of Acquisition Challenges and Opportunities

We also used our SME interviews to elicit perspectives on challenges and opportunities related to the acquisition of PAI capabilities.

Outcomes

Combined, these efforts produced a list of current COTS/GOTS PAI analytic tools; a taxonomy of needed PAI capabilities; and a set of findings on Army PAI needs, acquisition issues, and industry collaboration issues. These, in turn, drove a set of recommendations for ARCYBER and the Army to better acquire PAI analytic capabilities in a mostly proprietary commercial landscape.

Organization of This Report

The remainder of this report consists of four chapters. Chapter 2 looks at the analysis of current and needed PAI capabilities and requirements. Chapter 3 describes challenges and opportunities in the acquisition of PAI capabilities. Chapter 4 covers publicly available datasets. Chapter 5 provides our recommendations and describes research opportunities to further the development and acquisition of PAI tools and capabilities. The report also includes five appendixes. Appendix A provides the interview protocols. Appendix B contains the taxonomy of PAI needed capabilities. Appendix C provides visualizations from the PAI subcategory crosswalk by IRC. Appendix D provides the scenarios used in the scenario-based workshops. Appendix E provides a taxonomy of data.

CHAPTER 2

Current and Needed PAI Capabilities and Requirements

To better understand the Army's current PAI capabilities and requirements for PAI, as well as barriers and enablers to agile, effective acquisition of capabilities (both data and tools), our team sought to compare the *needs* (what the Army needs to be able to do in this space) with the *capabilities* (the tools the Army currently uses or that are available in the commercial and governmental marketplace). In the gap analysis, we also considered the challenges, barriers, and enablers related to closing identified gaps.

Inventorying Available COTS/GOTS PAI Capabilities and Army Requirements

Our effort to understand the gap between current Army PAI capabilities and requirements began with the identification of existing PAI capabilities; we then proceeded with an enumeration of Army requirements for PAI capabilities.

We first sought to identify existing COTS/GOTS PAI capabilities, excluding piloted-but-not-operationalized demonstrations from the academic and research world, as described in the Approach section in Chapter 1. From this effort, we identified a candidate list of 314 PAI tools and platforms, from boutique software tools to large, integrated vertical applications covering broad capability areas.

Using this list of potentially relevant tools, our next step was to systematically identify requirements for analyzing PAI across Army missions. The result of this effort was a categorized taxonomy of requirements with five main categories, 19 subcategories, and 172 discrete tasks. We then examined the gap between available capabilities and requirements.

Figure 2.1 shows the five categories of Army requirements for PAI capabilities that we identified, which can be defined as follows:

- *sense*: identifying, collecting, and preparing PAI data
- *understand*: the various methods and technology for turning raw data into insight
- *plan*: PAI-informed operations planning
- *assess*: using PAI to assess operations

FIGURE 2.1
Categories of Army Requirements for PAI Capabilities

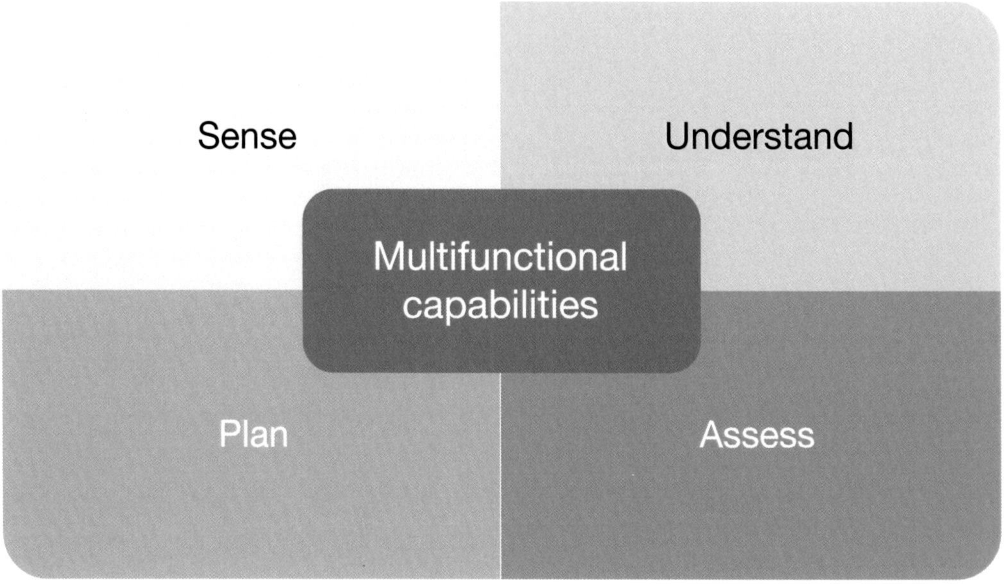

- *multifunctional capabilities*: capabilities that are multifunctional and foundational to all PAI analysis.

Table 2.1 shows the subcategories within each of these categories and provides examples of the capabilities in each. Table 2.2. addresses the same for the multifunctional capabilities. The full taxonomy is shown in Appendix B.

Multifunctional Capabilities: The Foundation for PAI Analytics

As we decomposed PAI analytic tasks, it quickly became clear that some capabilities, such as machine learning estimators, visualization, and network analysis, did not fit in a single category of the sense, understand, plan, and assess process for PAI analytics. These capabilities instead enabled other categories and are foundational to PAI analytics overall. There are nine core capabilities that enable the full range of PAI analytic tasks. These capabilities are especially critical because they are useful to all Army informational forces using PAI. These multifunctional capabilities are listed in Table 2.2.

Scenario Analysis

In addition to this taxonomy, our scenario-based analysis helped us better understand the Army's needs for the various PAI capabilities and activities in our taxonomy. The scenarios illustrated the kinds of investments in PAI capabilities that will be needed in the cur-

TABLE 2.1

Examples of Requirements for PAI in Four Overarching Categories

Category	Subcategories and Examples of Discrete Tasks
Sense	• *Gather and ingest* (e.g., ingest multimedia, dark/deep web scraping, remote sensing, public records, logistics data, survey and polling databases, market intelligence) • *Clean* (e.g., different types of media cleaning, error detection, image denoising) • *Index, process, and organize* (e.g., source characterization, anonymization, data enrichment, archive) • *Consolidate and merge* (e.g., consolidation, integration with other information sources, records matching)
Understand	• *Explore and describe* (e.g., summarization, media monitoring, data exploration or manipulation) • *Detect, identify, and analyze relevant individuals and groups* (e.g., audience, group, or individual analysis; coordinated activity identification) • *Detect, identify, and analyze relevant topics* (e.g., topic detection, relevance scoring, influence scoring, inauthentic material detection, authentic material verification, content tracking monitoring) • *Prediction, indication, and warning* (e.g., detection and alerts of emergent or concerning events and threats in the information environment; thresholding, predictive analytics, and forecasting)
Plan	• Standard military planning tasks • Digital information environment (IE) sandbox • Analytical tasks included elsewhere are also relevant here
Assess	• Standard military assessment tasks • Monitoring response to stimulus (e.g., changes because of U.S. presence/operations, changes because of adversary presence/operations) • Analytical tasks included elsewhere are also relevant here

TABLE 2.2

Multifunctional Capabilities

Subcategory	Examples
GIS	Geo-inferencing, spatial overlays, sociocultural overlays
Machine translation	Automated speech transcription, translation
Vision and biometrics	Visual object/entity recognition, facial recognition
Social science modeling	Behavioral analysis, social prediction
Narrative and discourse analysis	Narrative identification and analysis, sentiment and stance analysis
Visualization	Networks, geospatial, common operating picture
Machine learning	Classification and clustering, document similarity, segmentation
Network analysis	Community detection, information flow, centrality measures
Natural language processing (NLP)	Entity detection and enrichment, corpus analysis, text segmentation

rent operating environment. The global information environment is a contested space, with America's enemies engaged in multiple malign influence efforts. The scenarios showed that, as U.S. Army forces operate across the globe, PAI analytics are vital for planning, operations, and assessment across a range of operations, including PA, MISO, CA, cyber, intelligence, military deception, and operations security.[1] Appendix C provides visualizations of the information capability requirements by PAI based on the scenario analyses.

Gap Analysis

Our final step in this part of the analysis was to crosswalk the analytic requirements we identified in the previous subsection and listed in Appendix B against our inventory of COTS/GOTS solutions and capabilities. It was beyond the scope of our project to field test the 314 COTS/GOTS tools in our inventory. We cannot say how effective any tool is, nor could we measure how any single tool covers the Army's capacity needs.

As an intermediate step, we individually decomposed the capabilities for each of the PAI tools in our inventory, matching them against the 19 subcategories of PAI capability requirements. This allowed us to measure the relative level of coverage across the range of PAI activities (the number of tools that include visualization, biometrics, GIS, assessment capabilities, etc., divided by the total number of tools).

Figure 2.2 shows the relative levels of industry and government investment in capability development, organized by our 19 subcategories of PAI activities. As indicated by the figure, current COTS/GOTS PAI capability is uneven. For example, 83 percent of the tools we inventoried can gather and ingest data, while only 6 percent of tools have any social science modeling capabilities. So, for example, in Figure 2.2, readers can see on the far left that more than 80 percent of the tools we inventoried have some capability to gather and ingest data, while, at the other end, less than 10 percent of the tools we inventoried had any social science modeling relevance. The lack of COTS/GOTS solutions for nine of the 19 major PAI subcategory capabilities we identified represents a capability gap for the force.

Using the above distributions, we split the existing tools inventoried into three ordinal categories: (relatively) high, medium, and low coverage. Subcategories covered by 50 percent or more of the tools inventoried were counted as *high*, between 50 percent and 30 percent as *medium*, and 30 percent or below as *low*. Thus, we could identify, at a meso-level of granularity, which capabilities are more or less available through COTS/GOTS solutions.

Our criteria for deciding whether any given tool covered a subtype were *availability* and *evidence of capability*. To count something as COTS/GOTS, the tool had to be commercially available or operationally in use by government, and so we excluded proofs of concepts and developmental (but not yet deployed) technology. We also looked for evidence supporting

---

[1] This finding arose from our scenario analysis, which revealed the additional capability areas needing and using PAI for their specific missions (DoDD 3115.18, 2020).

FIGURE 2.2
Army PAI Needs Subcategories by Amount of Coverage

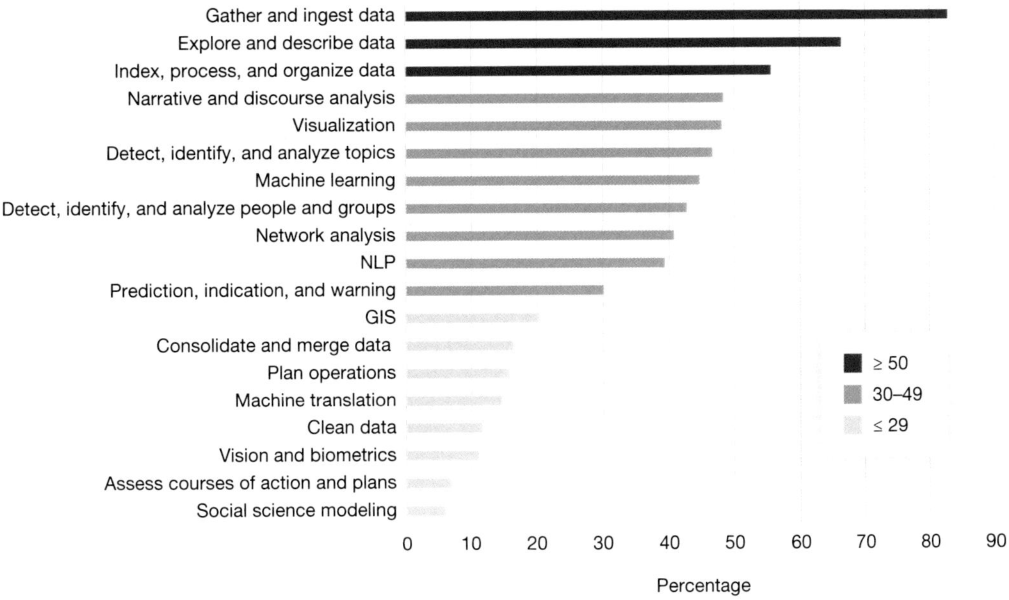

capability claims—it is one thing for marketing to claim that a given product is language agnostic, but quite another to demonstrate that. We thus counted a capability claim only when we could find published research, capability demonstrations, or detailed methodological explanations that plausibly supported such claims. Finally, we did not include commercial or nonprofit organizations' analytic services as off-the-shelf tools.

Table 2.3 breaks down the low-, medium-, and high-coverage capabilities with illustrative examples of specific tasks within each.

We repeat our caveat that we did not consider capacity requirements. So, for example, while gathering and ingesting as a subcategory has relatively high coverage compared with computer vision and biometrics, that might reflect that the former is more broadly necessary to PAI analytics and the latter is more of a niche category. After consideration of that limitation, we believe that low coverage for capabilities is a useful signal for considering deliberate investment and development by the Army—or, because those areas likely have capability gaps. For example, four subcategories are both multifunctional and relatively low in coverage: GIS, machine translation, vision and biometrics, and social science modeling. These are likely critical for Army investment and development.

Table 2.4 breaks down low-, medium-, and high-capability applicability across the Army by IRC.

Our applicability rankings add further context in that capabilities that are less covered by existing solutions and also widely applicable might provide the highest ROI for the Army.

TABLE 2.3

Low-, Medium-, and High-Coverage Capabilities

Subcategory	Examples	Coverage Level
Prediction, indication, and warning	Early warning, predictive analytics, threat assessment	Low
GIS	Geo-inferencing, spatial overlays, sociocultural overlays	Low
Consolidate and merge data	Merge data, join data, crossplatform linking	Low
Plan operations	IE sandbox, influence operations planning	Low
Machine translation	Automated speech transcription, translation	Low
Clean data	Ad stripping, deduplication, text encoding cleaning	Low
Vision and biometrics	Visual object/entity recognition, facial recognition	Low
Assess courses of action and plans	Engagement and effectiveness assessment, offline response monitoring	Low
Social science modeling	Behavioral analysis, social prediction	Low
Narrative and discourse analysis	Narrative ID/analysis, sentiment and stance analysis	Medium
Visualization	Networks, geospatial, common operating picture	Medium
Detect, identify, and analyze topics	Topic detection, influence scoring, fake detection	Medium
Machine learning	Classification/clustering, document similarity, segmentation	Medium
Detect, identify, and analyze people and groups	Audience analysis, social listening, pattern of life analysis	Medium
Network analysis	Community detection, information flow, centrality measures	Medium
NLP	Entity detection/enrichment, corpus analysis, text segmentation	Medium
Gather and ingest data	SM, web, and dark/deep web scraping, users-as-sensors	High
Explore and describe data	Query/filter, sort, summarize	High
Index, process, and organize data	Index, anonymize, enrich, normalize, organize	High

One capability in particular, PAI for prediction, indication, and warning, is both low coverage and high applicability, and thus investment into and development of that capability might produce high value across the Army.

Given all the above, we think our analysis has some degree of error at the level of any single tool—doubtless there are some that have capabilities for which we did not have evidence, and likewise some capabilities might not, in practice, be as robust as a research paper or demonstration claims. Our hope, though, is that the analysis is robust and useful at the aggregate

TABLE 2.4
Low-, Medium-, and High-Capability Applicability

Subcategory	Examples	Coverage Level
Prediction, indication, and warning	Early warning, predictive analytics, threat assessment	High
Network analysis	Community detection, information flow, centrality measures	High
Visualization	Networks, geospatial, common operating picture	High
Detect, identify, and analyze people and groups	Audience analysis, social listening, pattern of life analysis	High
Explore and describe data	Query/filter, sort, summarize	High
Gather and ingest data	SM, web, and dark/deep web scraping, users-as-sensors	High
Narrative and discourse analysis	Narrative ID/analysis, sentiment and stance analysis	High
GIS	Geo-inferencing, spatial overlays, sociocultural overlays	Medium
Detect, identify, and analyze topics	Topic detection, influence scoring, fake detection	Medium
Index, process, and organize data	Index, anonymize, enrich, normalize, organize	Medium
NLP	Entity detection/enrichment, corpus analysis, text segmentation	Medium
Machine learning	Classification/clustering, document similarity, segmentation	Medium
Vision and iometrics	Visual object/entity recognition, facial recognition	Medium
Assess courses of action and plans	Engagement and effectiveness assessment, offline response monitoring	Medium
Social science modeling	Behavioral analysis, social prediction	Low
Machine translation	Automated speech transcription, translation	Low
Plan operations	Information environment sandbox, influence ops planning	Low

level; that, for example, visualization really is moderately covered by existing COTS/GOTS tools, gathering and ingesting is indeed well-covered, and social science modeling capabilities, in fact, have low coverage.

Conclusion

This analysis helps establish and document the necessity for a robust U.S. Army PAI analytics capability. To execute a variety of missions in the information age, the Army needs to be able to gather and ingest a wide array of PAI data, make sense of that data, use that sense-making to inform planning, and then assess and refine those plans in data-centric ways. As shown in this chapter, there is a meaningful gap between current capabilities in existing tools and needed PAI capabilities across a range of Army missions—the majority of existing tools go after the lowest-hanging fruit. Furthermore, while existing COTS/GOTS solutions might close some of this gap, there are capabilities that need to be developed or customized to meet mission needs.[2] And, as noted by one of our interview participants, because PAI capabilities are a nascent, quick-developing field, we can expect additional requirements to emerge.[3]

In the next chapter, we discuss some issues surrounding an acquisition strategy for PAI capabilities.

---

[2] U.S. military officer with expertise in information warfare, telephone interview with the authors, January 26, 2022.

[3] U.S. military and Army civilian employees involved in Army acquisitions, telephone interview with the authors, April 8, 2022. Additionally, DoDD 3115.18 recognizes the fluid nature of PAI analytics, which is why it directs the Under Secretary of Defense for Research and Engineering to facilitate the rapid development and prototyping of these capabilities and Under Secretary of Defense for Acquisition and Sustainment to support sustainment for PAI tools for both the services' and DoD needs. Please see Appendix B for a taxonomy of those needs.

CHAPTER 3

Challenges and Opportunities in the Acquisition of PAI Capabilities

There are several challenges to acquiring PAI capabilities, including commercial incentives against flexibility and advantageous pricing for the Army, cultural and knowledge barriers to collaboration with industry, uneven development across capabilities, and the lack of a program of record that supports enterprise-level acquisition efficiencies.

These are, however, challenges the Army can meet. The Army can leverage its existing development and acquisition structures and programs to efficiently build its PAI analytic capacity. There are many Army entities, such as United States Army Special Operations Command, the Combined Arms Center, and Department of the Army Management Office—Strategic Operations, that need to be better aligned to develop capabilities that leverage PAI. However, ARCYBER's central position within the various informational functions can act as a hub and proponent for PAI analytics. Finally, the Army has sufficient flexibility in acquisition to balance cost efficiency with agility in a dynamic and evolving set of technologies.

This chapter describes some challenges and opportunities related to the acquisition of PAI capabilities. These findings are drawn largely from our semi-structured interviews with Army and industry personnel.

Acquisition of PAI Analytic Capabilities

The Army needs an enterprise acquisition strategy for PAI that is flexible. Interview SMEs pointed out that the dynamic nature of PAI analytics means that any acquisition approach must retain flexibility. On one hand, economies of scale in purchasing improve U.S. government leverage in negotiating with industry, allowing category management efforts to improve ROI and prevent waste and duplication.[1] On the other hand, emerging operational requirements and differing planning horizons across various echelons require agile procurement

[1] U.S. Army civilian employees with acquisition expertise, telephone interview with the authors, March 25, 2022.

strategies to meet immediate needs.[2] This flexibility might include program manager use of support contracts so that operational units can get timely support.[3]

Program Executive Office (PEO) Enterprise Information Systems (EIS) is the likeliest location for an enterprise-level PAI data and analytics program. SMEs indicated that, given its enterprise focus, PEO EIS is a more logical location for an enterprise-level PAI data and analytics program than PEO Intelligence Electronic Warfare and Sensors with its tactical focus. Within PEO EIS, the Computer Hardware, Enterprise Software and Solutions (CHESS) program is responsible for procuring COTS software and services and thus is the closest program match for PAI capabilities. CHESS, however, does not cover data acquisition and might be oriented toward traditional information technology (IT) capabilities that are not as dynamic as PAI capabilities development.[4]

There are existing programs and models across the joint force for supporting agile scaling and defense acquisition of new technologies. Examples of this include Defense Innovation Units; other transaction authorities, such as the Army's Cornerstone Consortium; and incubator-style programs, such as the Army Applications Lab and X-Tech Search, the Cyber Fusion Innovation Center, and the Air Force's AFWERX nonprofit program.[5] Such programs can function as scaffolding, bringing together stakeholders from DoD, industry, and academia, helping coordinate and support innovation for defense acquisition.

The Marine Corps' model for PAI analytics might be useful for the U.S. Army. The Marine Corps' model has a service-level proponent for PAI analytics (the Marine Corps Information Operations Center) that coordinates acquisition for PAI tools but also provides reach-back support when operational units need specialized support.[6] Having a PAI proponent has been critical for successes in navigating the legal, administrative, and technical challenges of gathering and analyzing PAI for broad service use.[7] This organization acquires PAI tools and capabilities, but also acts as a clearing house so that multiple Marine Corps organizations are not procuring PAI tools on an ad-hoc basis. It helps deconflict multiple

---

[2] U.S. military officer in cyber operations, telephone interview with the authors, June 16, 2022; U.S. military officers and Army civilian employee with expertise in technology, telephone interview with the authors, July 8, 2022.

[3] U.S. military and Army civilian employees involved in Army acquisition, telephone interview with the authors, April 8, 2022.

[4] Army civilian employees with acquisition expertise, telephone interview with the authors, April 4, 2022; U.S. military officers with expertise in program execution, telephone interview with the authors, July 8, 2022.

[5] U.S. military and Army civilian employees involved in Army acquisition, telephone interview with the authors, April 8, 2022.

[6] Originally established under the Deputy Commandant for Plans, Policies, and Operations. For more details, see Francis K. Chawk, "Marine Corps Information Operations Center," *Marine Corps Gazette*, April 2020.

[7] U.S. military officers with expertise in PAI analytics, telephone interview with the authors, March 4, 2022.

requests from Marine Corps organizations for the same PAI tools, but also acts as a conduit for acquisition.

Collaboration with Industry

Knowledge Gaps

There are knowledge gaps within DoD when collaborating with commercial tech vendors. Coherent data strategies and standards, like those for application programming interfaces, are not always readily available upon request for vendors, and, often, there is no one available to engage with regarding technical specifications.[8]

There is a knowledge gap within the industry on the U.S. Army's mission. Multiple times throughout the interview process, commercial interviewees expressed industry concerns about working with DoD. Within the PAI analytics space, this often involves privacy concerns and implications for sharing data or services with the Army, especially regarding the well-being of American citizens. Such concerns reflect a lack of trust or understanding in the Army's principles and mission (i.e., the Army focuses on malign, foreign threats), highlighting an inaccurate public perception of the Army in this area.[9]

Partnerships

Industry's willingness to collaborate and be flexible will depend in part on the type of firm. Defense contractors are generally flexible working with DoD; dual-use commercial firms might be willing to work with DoD to the degree that their existing products and services can be used as-is.[10]

Established, DoD-centric vendors are more flexible and amenable to the Army's requests to maintain the overall relationship. For large prime contractors, flexibility allows for the commercialization of the requested capability and ultimately creates a new revenue stream for the vendor.[11]

Dependence on a single platform or vendor presents risk to the Army. While established, ongoing relationships have benefits, a single-source vendor might mean the Army becomes dependent on that partner. This might create risk. For example, the Army might find that it has to choose between (1) enforcing a requirement to scan a solution or platform

8 Industry experts in SM analytics, telephone interview with the authors, March 28, 2022.

9 Industry experts in information operations, telephone interview with the authors, November 11, 2021.

10 Industry analytics experts, telephone interview with the authors, November 11, 2021; Industry experts in SM analytics, telephone interview with the authors, March 28, 2022.

11 Industry experts in SM analytics, telephone interview with the authors, March 28, 2022.

for vulnerabilities that is proprietary or black box (or has proprietary elements) or (2) losing access to the platform.[12]

Startups face a variety of challenges in collaborating with the Army. Multiple SMEs pointed out that contracting compliance might be a barrier to working with DoD.[13] Startups might have the exact solution to an Army problem, but the slow pace of the contracting process gets in the way.[14] Other potential barriers for startups include having to be subs for larger, prime contractors, which reduces startup profit margins; challenges forecasting revenue with DoD contracting; and the risk of becoming dependent on the government as a sole or primary revenue source.[15] When a provider supplies only data or analytics, there is less connectivity and feedback, and the vendor no longer has any access to or control over how the data are used or whether the vendor is violating any agreements with its data suppliers; this creates business risk for the vendor and lessens its competitive edge.

Economic Barriers and Incentives

Revenue is the primary incentive for industry partnerships. There is an opportunity cost associated with addressing the military market. Industry personnel emphasized that, when government requests flexibility from industry—unbundling capabilities, access to data behind platforms or services, customization—companies might expect or need the government to pay for the equivalent commercial loss.[16] This is particularly true for startups.[17]

Startup costs might be a barrier to many of the efficiencies and options from which the Army would benefit. Industry analytic experts noted that switching from individual licenses to an organizational license has costs associated with group authentication that would need to be paid upfront to get lower ongoing cost savings.[18]

The Army will have to pay for any specific capabilitiy it might want. Often, smaller companies have the exact capability the Army is requesting, but, because of the budget process and the fast pace of the tech space, these companies do not want to take on the risk of going under by specializing their solutions for a DoD client. If the tool requested cannot also

---

[12] Industry experts on knowledge systems, telephone interview with the authors, March 2, 2022.

[13] Industry experts in information operations, telephone interview with the authors, October 25, 2021; Industry experts in information operations, telephone interview with the authors, November 11, 2021.

[14] Retired U.S. military officer with expertise in PAI analytics, telephone interview with the authors, November 12, 2021.

[15] Industry experts in government contracting, telephone interview with the authors, December 7, 2021.

[16] Industry experts in artificial intelligence and analytics, telephone interview with the authors, October 19, 2021; Industry experts in SM, telephone interview with the authors, October 21, 2021; Industry experts in information operations, telephone interview with the authors, November 11, 2021; Group semi-structured interview with industry personnel, telephone interview with the authors, November 30, 2021.

[17] Industry experts in SM analytics, telephone interview with the authors, March 28, 2022.

[18] Industry experts in SM analytics, telephone interview with the authors, March 28, 2022.

be commercialized for the private sector, then companies might expect or need the government to pay for the equivalent commercial loss. Additionally, startups face revenue losses working under a prime contractor, the inability to forecast revenue, and high risks should a contract be voided.[19]

Data and tools might have distinct value propositions and thus require different acquisition approaches. For analytics vendors, built-in costs to disaggregate components are likely to be a barrier to flexible acquisition: It is simply easier to sell integrated platforms as is.[20] For data providers, there are few costs associated with sharing all or part of their data. Social and business risk in selling to DoD is a more likely barrier to acquisition.[21]

Conclusion

In this chapter, we identified a variety of challenges associated with the acquisition of PAI capabilities. These include the need for the Army to develop a strategy for acquiring PAI and challenges related to establishing partnerships with industry, addressing pricing and costs, and overcoming knowledge barriers to collaboration. In the next chapter, we discuss publicly available datasets before presenting our recommendations in Chapter 5.

---

[19] Industry experts in information operations, telephone interview with the authors, November 11, 2021.

[20] Industry experts in disinformation and misinformation, telephone interview with the authors, March 3, 2022; Industry experts in disinformation and misinformation, telephone interview with the authors, March 8, 2022.

[21] Industry experts in disinformation and misinformation, telephone interview with the authors, March 3, 2022.

CHAPTER 4

Publicly Available Datasets

Background

In addition to available COTS/GOTS analytic tools, we considered the universe of PAI datasets and how they might relate to the Army's needs. We considered three varieties. First, government entities collect some datasets (for example, the Bureau of Economic Analysis [BEA] collects and publishes a variety of economic transactions). Second, many datasets can be purchased either from nonspecialist companies (for example, employment websites often offer data about open job positions) or specialist companies (for example, data brokers). Third, some datasets are collected and made freely available by individuals or private entities. Although the quality of these datasets can vary, the most notable sources often are extensive in coverage and of high quality.

In the rest of this chapter, we present a PAI data acquisition model (supply) and dataset evaluation criteria. We also present a PAI data usage model (demand), including contexts for PAI data usage and considerations for the characteristics of data. Appendix E presents a detailed taxonomy of PAI data types that can inform data acquisition and usage in support of the Army's missions in accordance with this chapter's discussion.

Matching Data Supply to Demand

As an organization considers its data needs, one useful model to consider is how the available supply of data matches up with the organization's expected demand for data. Figure 4.1 illustrates this relationship. As the figure demonstrates, many factors can affect the need for data (demand) and the amount of available data, which is useful for analyzing a specific need (supply). On the supply side, such factors as the number of sources of data and the variety of data each source can provide will expand or contract the overall supply of data. On the demand side, such factors as the purpose of the data or the type of user (academic, governmental, commercial, etc.) can affect the value of the data for the intended consumer. While the specific examples illustrated in Figure 4.1 are only a few ways the characteristics of data supply and demand can affect the value users derive from data, this figure illustrates how

FIGURE 4.1
Dimensions of the Taxonomy of Data

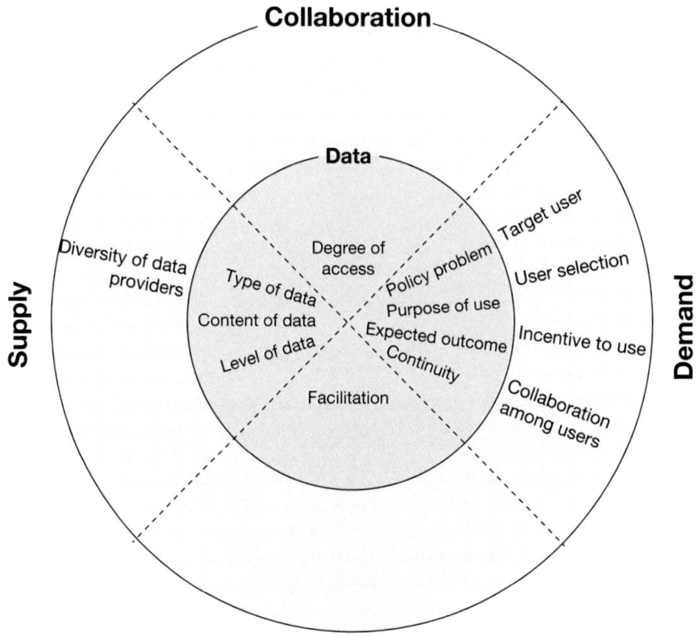

SOURCE: Reproduced from Iryna Susha, Marijn Janssen, and Stefaan Verhulst, "Data Collaboratives as a New Frontier of Cross-Sector Partnerships in the Age of Open Data: Taxonomy Development," *Proceedings of the 50th Hawaii International Conference on System Sciences*, January 2017, p. 2696.

both supply and demand of data need to be taken into account for an organization to derive the maximum value from the data available to it.

In short, when analyzing complex information environments, the value of the data is defined by how well the data's supply meets the mission demand. The quality of each is important for ensuring effective mission analysis and for conducting operations. In the following sections, we outline a supply and demand taxonomy for data. The taxonomy is drawn from a mixture of practitioner experience, business intelligence literature, and IT best practices. In the next section, we examine the supply side, with a focus on how aggregating governmental, commercial, and open data sources can leverage PAI for a variety of Army missions.

Supply

One approach to characterizing data supply is to group it according to key characteristics. The goal is an information equilibrium where the quality of information is sufficient to meet the demand generated by the mission requirements. For the supply side of data, organizations should take note of three characteristics: quality, source type, and scope. The next sections explore each of these dataset qualities in more detail.

Data Quality Characteristics

Data quality includes the attributes and characteristics of the data that affect its overall value for analysis. The biggest challenge with developing high-quality data is the risk that the data being captured are inaccurate or lack key information to make an operational decision. For example, false positives are a critical concern. There are many ways to measure the quality of data sources within the data supply. One approach is to use evaluative quality characteristics known as the *5Vs* of data quality:[1]

- *value*: the cost-benefit result of using, accessing, and storing the data source
- *volume*: the data source's size, both in number of records and data storage requirements
- *velocity*: how quickly data are generated and how quickly those data can be made available for analysis
- *variety*: the diversity of data sources and data types (structured, unstructured, or semi-structured)
- *veracity*: the representativeness of the data and how "true" the data are as compared with the original source (source truth decay is an issue that should be considered).[2]

By systematically classifying data sources by these quality characteristics, the overall quality of the data supply can be determined. For example, if the mission called for evaluating SM history and credit card purchases, then we could use the 5Vs to qualitatively evaluate the relevance of datasets purchased through a data broker. We might purchase data about an individual's use of Twitter to get a user's SM history as well as data about their recent credit card purchases. The Twitter dataset could have a series of posts that describe behavior associated with protests. If the SM data show high veracity and volume, and the credit card dataset shows a high velocity of transactions for goods that are useful for protesting (such as face coverings, rags, and protective gear), a probable model could be more believable than if one or more of the data sources did not demonstrate the 5V characteristics.

Source Type Characteristics

The origin of data can have important effects on the availability and quality of those data. For PAI, we group the source *types* of data into four broad categories:

---

[1] Ishwarappa and J. Anuradha, "A Brief Introduction on Big Data 5Vs Characteristics and Hadoop Technology," *Procedia Computer Science*, Vol. 48, 2015.

[2] Francesco Cappa, Raffaele Oriani, Enzo Peruffo, and Ian McCarthy, "Big Data for Creating and Capturing Value in the Digitalized Environment: Unpacking the Effects of Volume, Variety, and Veracity on Firm Performance," *Journal of Product Innovation Management*, Vol. 38, No. 1, January 2021.

- *crowdsourced data*: data created or curated by private individuals or groups of private individuals
- *commercial data*: data collected and held by private companies
- *public and administrative data*: data collected and held by domestic government agencies, states, and public organizations (e.g., community organizations)
- *international data*: data collected and held by international agents, nation-states, non-state actors, multinational corporations, and international organizations.

These types of datasets vary in two important respects. First, the quality and reliability of the dataset will vary depending on the trustworthiness of the organization or individuals collecting the data. Information collected by U.S. official government agencies is usually considered authoritative and reliable. The quality of information collected by private-sector actors—whether companies or individuals—can vary to a greater degree. Second, the origin of data can affect the cost. Crowdsourced data or data obtained from an official government source are typically free to acquire; however, the receiving organization might have to invest some of its own resources to process the data into a form suitable for analysis. Commercial data will typically require a payment from the receiving organization to acquire but might require less data engineering to make the data useful for analysis.

Data Scope Characteristics

To further characterize the available data, we grouped them based on their *scope*. By this we mean data scoped to the individual and group levels:

- *nationally identified data (NID)*: data organized at a group level with emphasis on national importance or effect
- *personally identified data (PID)*: data organized at the individual level with an emphasis on personal importance or effect.

Differentiating the data in this way helps us group them by their likely use case. Data focused on individuals can often be used together. For example, datasets describing the demographic characteristics of individuals (where they live, how old they are, etc.) are often combined with datasets describing the interests of those individuals (likes horror movies, plays a particular sport, etc.). In contrast, datasets focused on larger groups are not useful for microtargeting (i.e., when an organization promotes the same overall end goal for a messaging campaign by sending different messages tailored to individuals based on their personal characteristics). Instead, NID are more commonly used to identify larger trends. For example, NID might identify changes in automobile traffic flows or in the amount of foot traffic at a particular point of interest.

When we put these three sets of characteristics together, we can list examples of data types by mission requirement. The interaction of these three values helps determine whether an associated supplied dataset is sufficient for an information transaction. In short, as we continue to develop a supply-demand model for information transactions relevant to Army operations, the model will get better at defining what quality, type, and scope of data is most useful for the variety of Army missions.

Data Taxonomy

Given this context, Appendix E presents a detailed taxonomy of the kinds of PAI datasets that might be available. This taxonomy is the amalgamation of several data catalogs available in the private sector; it includes the kinds of data available for purchase from data brokers, for targeted digital advertising, and from government or noncommercial entities. Appendix E provides details about the data sources used to construct this taxonomy.

Demand

Although understanding the breadth and variety of publicly available data is important, it is equally important to focus on how the Army might make use of those data to support its essential mission. To guide our analysis, we leveraged the five scenarios used in other parts of this research to illustrate a variety of information-relevant Army missions. Such missions include

- protecting the Army's reputation and brand from disinformation
- force protection from such threats as workplace violence or extremist attacks
- providing threat warning for global events
- understanding sentiment among the population in areas where the Army is conducting stability operations
- supporting information operations against hostile regimes.

Appendix D includes hypothetical scenarios illustrating each of these missions. There are two types of considerations when thinking about the demand for data: the context and categories of data. We explain both of those next.

Data Contexts

Placing the Army's data needs in the context of these scenarios can help the Army understand which dimensions of the supply of PAI data would be most relevant given the expected way the Army intends to use the data. For example, where the Army intends to operate will have a substantial effect on the kinds of data it can leverage. The Army's intended operation locations can be broadly categorized into four groups:

- U.S. homeland
- allied or friendly
- neutral or contested
- adversary.

At one end of this spectrum, the Army is legally prohibited from obtaining or using most data about U.S. citizens. Even when data can be legally obtained and used, it might be inadvisable to do so because of the potential backlash from the U.S. public. Similarly, while the Army might not be legally prohibited from collecting and using some kinds of data in friendly countries, the Army would most likely not want to operate in ways that might provoke a significant backlash from the publics of those countries. At the same time, the potential to use data is often greatest at this end of the spectrum. Typically, more data are collected in wealthier countries, and U.S. citizens usually have the greatest cultural familiarity with their own country and with its closest allies, increasing the likelihood that the Army's message will resonate with its target audience.

At the other end of the spectrum, the U.S. military has the fewest legal, practical, or ethical barriers to acquiring and operationalizing data for influence operations either against hostile governments or in support of warfighting and stabilization operations conducted abroad. At the same time, the digital infrastructure to collect data will vary greatly across these environments, and the U.S. military might have difficulty purchasing or acquiring datasets in these locations. Similarly, U.S. military personnel might not be able to effectively interpret and use data from countries where they do not have a deep understanding of the cultural context.

Data Categories

Additionally, the Army should consider the kinds of data that would be most valuable to it in the context of its primary use cases for data. One common way that digital marketers separate data into types is by considering what kind of information the data provide about a person. They often group data into

- basic or identity data
- behavioral data
- attitudinal data.

Basic or identity data include typical demographic information, such as a person's age, gender, or place of residence. However, these data also include nondemographic information, such as the person's leisure interests, political affiliations, or employer. Essentially, these kinds of data are facts about a person.

Behavioral data, as the name implies, describe how the person acts. In a commercial context, these data typically center on how a person is interacting with the company's product or service. For noncommercial entities, such as the Army, these data will have a different focus. Instead, this kind of data could include pattern-of-life data from a person's day-to-day activities, such as location data showing where the person travels frequently, the relative intensity of their interest in a topic (does this person attend in-person protests or do they only share online content about the protest topic), and how they respond to outreach efforts as part of an information campaign (do they only read a post on SM or do they reshare and promote it, for example).

Finally, *attitudinal data* describes how people feel about a topic. Commercial businesses typically focus on how customers feel about their brand or their products. Although the Army does not offer products and services, it has an interest in understanding attitudes toward brands that are relevant to its interests. Domestically, the Army has a brand to protect and it will want to understand how potential recruits (and their parents, friends, and family) feel about them potentially joining the Army. Overseas, the Army might wish to monitor how citizens of a host nation feel about a U.S. Army presence or how individuals are perceiving an opposition movement to the government of an adversary. Depending on the Army's use case, different kinds of data will inform the Army in different ways and have different degrees of importance in helping it achieve its operational objectives.

Conclusion

Data captures nearly every aspect of an individual's life in the modern world. Although governments once owned the most comprehensive and authoritative datasets, businesses, organizations, and even entrepreneurial individuals now have the ability to create extensive and valuable caches of information. To avoid becoming overwhelmed by the ever-increasing volumes and varieties of available data, the Army should focus on matching its demand for data—the specific workflows and operations the Army needs to execute—against the available supply. This basic framework should allow the Army to expand its data universe beyond its familiar government-controlled sources and to fully utilize all the data-enhanced capabilities that will empower it to achieve information dominance.

CHAPTER 5

Recommendations and Conclusion

Developing a robust Army PAI analytics acquisition strategy and capability requires a strong organization to support the coordinated acquisition of PAI capabilities, strategic investments in those capabilities, and strong relationships between the Army and commercial industry. In this chapter, we present our recommendations to the Army for these issues.

Recommendations

Organization

The Army should designate a service-level PAI proponent to coordinate the Army's enterprise procurement and collaboration with industry. PAI analytics are a relatively new, dynamic set of capabilities. Furthermore, the activities that leverage PAI data and analysis (e.g., PSYOPS, PA, intelligence) are spread across the Army. Having a service-level voice (potentially ARCYBER) to act as a proponent for PAI acquisition will improve efficiencies and coordination.

The Army should designate PEO EIS as the most plausible location for an enterprise-level PAI data and analytics program. PEO EIS should be the program manager for PAI analytics acquisition. As the acquisition authority, PEO EIS would be able to work closely with the Army proponent for PAI analytics to define requirements and ensure timely and cost-efficient acquisition of PAI capabilities.

The Army should invest in personnel development for PAI analytics and the use of PAI data. The Army should invest in personnel who will enable collaboration between SMEs and personnel with technical and scientific skills who understand the data space and have technical expertise, research design skills, and mission understanding.[1] The Army should also consider how to leverage private-sector knowledge and experience in this area, such as existing private-sector resources on such topics as data-driven marketing, consumer behavior, and algorithmic marketing.

The Army should consider developing mission threads for PAI use in supporting Army missions and tasks. Ultimately, to get the most ROI, the Army needs to deeply understand the demand signal for how PAI-enhanced capabilities could help it accomplish its missions. By focusing its efforts on key workflows and understanding the purpose and intent

[1] Academic experts in information operations, telephone interview with the authors, October 25, 2021.

behind these workflows, the Army can best understand how they could be enhanced—or even transformed—using PAI-derived capabilities.

Strategic Capability Investment

The Army should prioritize investment in multifunctional capabilities that are foundational to PAI analytics, along with capabilities that are underrepresented in the current COTS/GOTS inventory. There are two kinds of capabilities in which the Army should consider prioritizing investment. Multifunctional capabilities, such as computer vision and biometrics or NLP, enable all the other kinds of capabilities the Army needs, and thus likely represent a high ROI for the Army. Investments should also be made in low-coverage capabilities—those capabilities in the bottom tranche of coverage for existing COTS/GOTS solutions. These critical but less-common capabilities represent another high-ROI for the Army. Finally, PAI for prediction and warning is both low coverage and high applicability, and thus investment into and development of that capability might produce high value across the Army.

The Army should collect internal analyst data with automated systems to better understand PAI analytic needs. Automated data collection of what datasets, tools, and platforms analysts use most can inform future procurement decisions and highlight system issues that need to be fixed. Then requirements from all parts of the organization can be collected so that a formal strategy for acquiring data and tools can be utilized when negotiating with vendors.[2]

Industry Collaboration

The Army should develop an acquisition strategy that facilitates collaboration with smaller companies. While startups are likely to have cutting-edge technology from which the Army can benefit, they face a variety of challenges in collaborating with the Army.[3] A scaffolding approach, like that of the Air Force's AFWERX, would allow for a distributed management structure with agile decisionmaking spread out (rather than top-down concentrated) and allow project managers to create flexible exit criteria as tools are built. Contracts and funding could still be managed in one location, helping smaller companies that are not experienced in collaborating with the Army. Additionally, a scaffolding approach could facilitate an accelerator program where startups are run in parallel cohorts so project performance data can be collected to inform decisions on which startup efforts should fail fast and which should be continued.

The Army might want to partner with digital marketing firms and advertising platforms to better understand industry best practices for leveraging PAI data. Given private-sector expertise in microtargeting and other digital persuasion techniques, collaboration

---

2 Industry experts in information operations, telephone interview with the authors, November 11, 2021.

3 Industry experts in venture capital, telephone interview with the authors, December 7, 2021.

with such partners might help the Army understand how to use such techniques effectively and accelerate the Army's ability to leverage cutting-edge targeting and marketing capabilities, as well as defend against them.

The Army should address industry concerns that it uses data and services unethically. This could include publishing clear PAI principles of conduct and ensuring that any vendors comply.[4] This could be done through a transparent internal review process that includes publication of an annual report stating how often vendors comply with law enforcement, types of products developed from the data, data breaches, etc.[5]

Conclusion

The process of acquiring PAI data sources and tools (that is, *PAI capabilities*), conducting analysis, and providing relevant outputs to multiple elements across the Army (and DoD) requires a coherent approach that leverages economies of scale. In this report, we have attempted to inform such a strategy. To help improve dissemination of our report's findings and recommendations, we have produced summary visual placemats as Figures 5.1 and 5.2.

Suggestions for Further Research

Over the course of this research, we identified multiple issues that would benefit from further investigation and analysis. For example, our GOTS/COTS analysis was at a medium level of granularity, and a more in-depth analysis of specific tools and capabilities could help direct investment and acquisition.

Furthermore, this Army-centric study did not address wider DoD coordination for PAI analytics. If the Army would benefit from a more consolidated, enterprise approach to acquainting PAI analytic capabilities and tools, it is likely that DoD would as well. Coordination across DoD, a common approach to acquisition, coordination in development and incubation, and common operating concepts and pictures are important areas for further study.

An additional, important analysis of this space would help government and military services better understand how best to leverage available PAI capabilities and methods. There would be considerable benefit to the Army in better understanding how to effectively and efficiently leverage PAI analytics to fulfill the Army's specific missions and requirements. As the Army moves toward implementation of its information advantage and multi-domain operations concepts, an understanding of how different PAI capabilities integrate to leverage the mountains of data being collected could help better operationalize these concepts.

---

[4] Industry experts in privacy and civil liberties, telephone interview with the authors, October 21, 2021.

[5] Industry experts in artificial intelligence and analytics, telephone interview with the authors, October 19, 2021.

FIGURE 5.1
Needed Army PAI Categories and Context

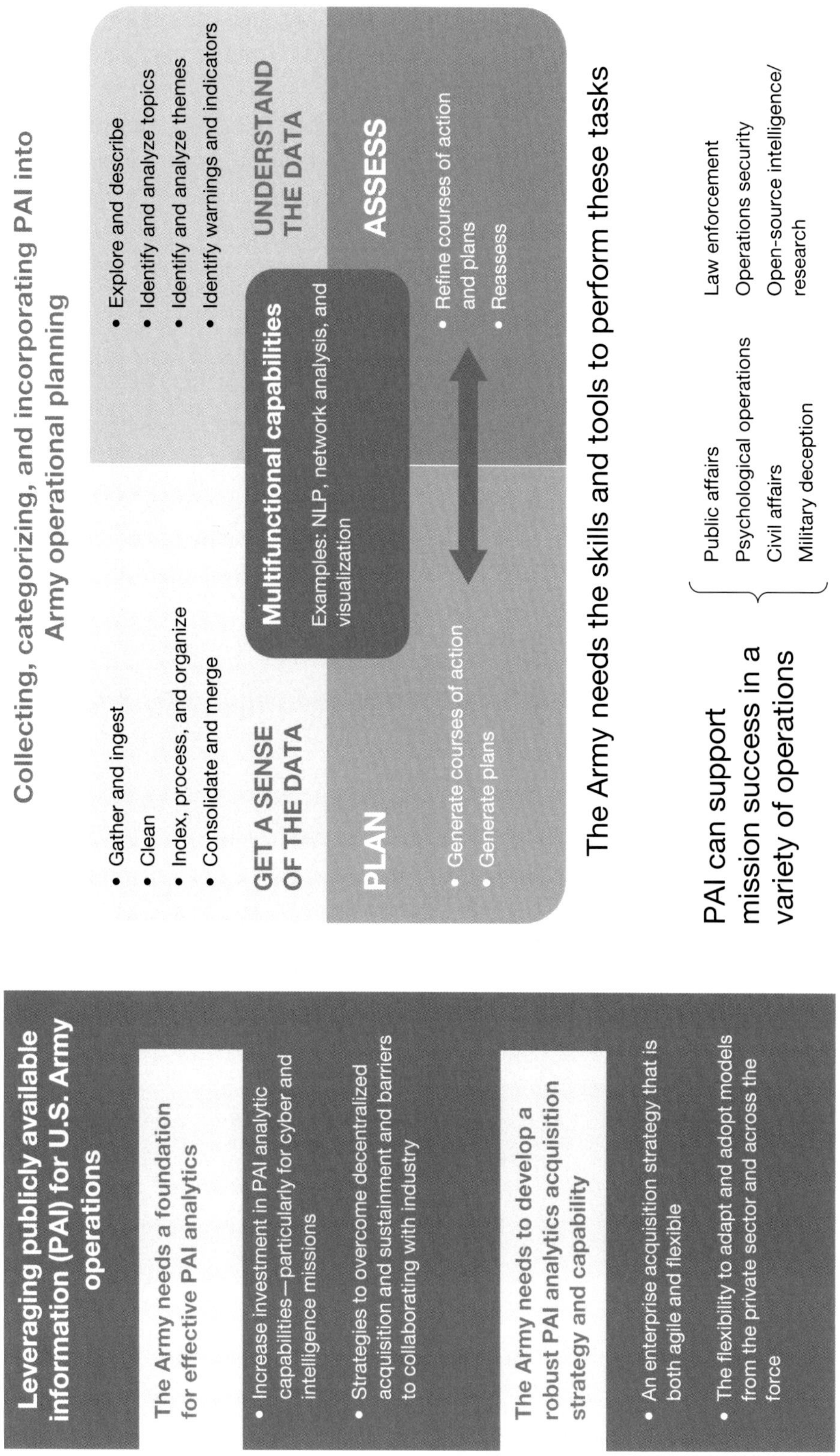

FIGURE 5.2
Required Army PAI Capability Gaps and Remediation Recommendations

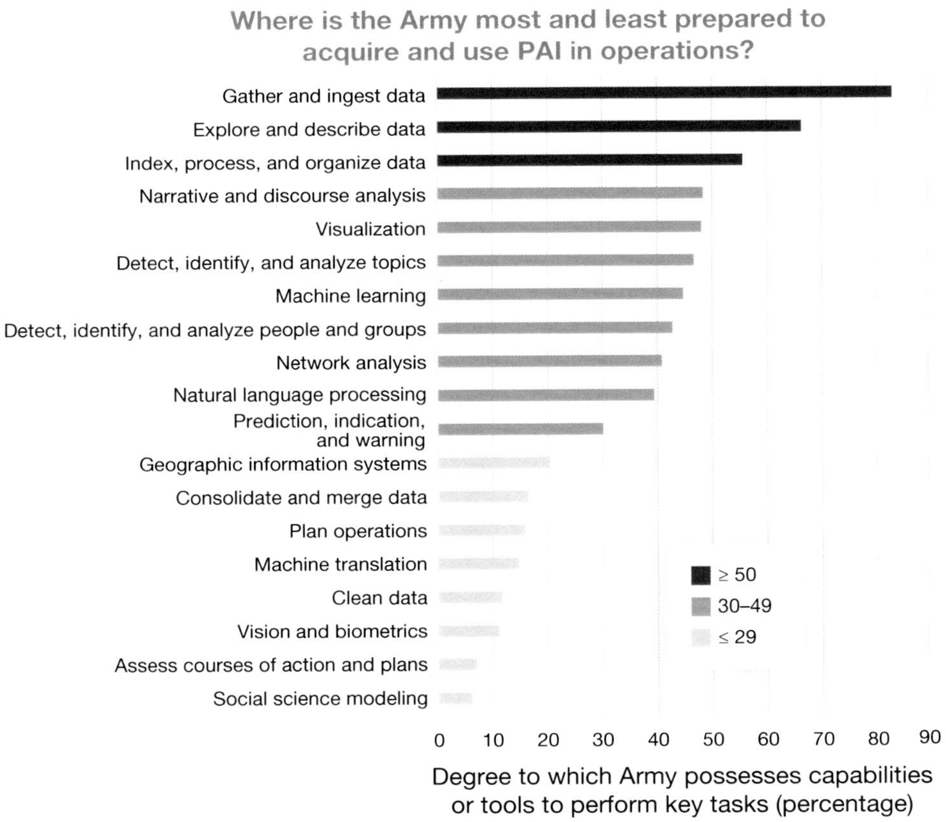

Future directions and next steps for U.S. Army Cyber Command

- **Increase investment in PAI analytic capabilities** to compete effectively in contested operating environments.
- **Adopt an enterprise approach** that streamlines and standardizes PAI capability procurement while promoting acquisition flexibility and agility in a dynamic technology field.
- **Leverage economies of scale** in PAI capability acquisition to improve pricing and ensure flexibility for industry partners.
- **Improve collaboration with industry**, including supporting non-prime contractors, and use multiple defense innovation acquisition resources.
- **Promote the Army's mission and ethical commitment** to PAI analytic capability development.
- **Designate a service-level PAI proponent** (possibly ARCYBER) to optimize the Army's enterprise procurement, flexibility and agility, and collaboration with industry.
- **Focus on multipurpose (universal) capabilities.** As part of an enterprise acquisition approach, start with universal capabilities, which are foundational to every other category. Rapidly develop a list of approved products and services and an exceptions request path to increase savings and flexibility for the most critical PAI capabilities.

APPENDIX A

Interview Protocols

This appendix includes two semi-structured interview protocols used during the RAND team's SME interviews. The first was used for our DoD and U.S. government (USG) interviews, which reflect the consumers of PAI analytics. The second protocol was used in interviewing industry suppliers of PAI analytics.

Protocol 1 (DoD/USG)

General Background Questions

1. Tell us about your role and the responsibilities of your current position.
2. How would you define publicly available information (PAI) and how does your organization use it? PAI is defined by DoDD 3115.18 as,
   - Information that has been published or broadcast for public consumption, is available on request to the public, is accessible online or otherwise to the public, is available to the public by subscription or purchase, could be seen or heard by a casual observer, is made available at a meeting open to the public, or is obtained by visiting a place or attending an event that is open to the public.

PAI is not intelligence; it is raw unanalyzed data. The Army has a very limited set of missions that utilize PAI. Similar to how there are firms who analyze foot traffic using location data to determine when a good time to reopen businesses during COVID, similar analyses could be done to provide the Army with early warnings of threats.

Capabilities and Tools

1. We want to understand some of the forward leaning ways to utilize PAI similar to how the private sector utilizes it. For example, marketing companies mine SM data for targeted advertisement. Similarly, the Army could utilize a similar SM process, combined with overhead imagery, to provide early warning of adversary military formation in Europe, Battle Damage Assessment, toxic exposure at a base. Can you tell me about any emerging artificial intelligence/machine learning (AI/ML) tools that you have to analyze PAI and for what purpose?
   a. What are the functions? How are they used? By whom?

   b. Are these capabilities leased/sold?
   c. What doesn't the current version of the tool do? What do you plan to do next with it?
   d. What current and future problem sets does your AI/ML capabilities address?
   e. What, if any, defense applications are there with your products/services?
2. How do you manage your PAI?
   a. What are some strategies or lessons learned for a centralized data framework? Analytics acquisition capability?
   b. Use Case principles? Privacy?
   c. Governance?
   d. Transparency?
3. What is the process that entities must undergo to partner with your organization for sharing and analyzing PAI?
   a. What is the structure in place to facilitate the sharing of PAI?
4. What are some restrictions on organizations that use your data/platform for defense applications?
   a. Purposes/data use agreements?
   b. Data storage limitations (duration, capacity, offsite/onsite storage)?
   c. Analysis restrictions?
5. How could the Army build trust with commercial partners and private sector that what they are doing is legitimate and appropriate? What would accountability/transparency look like?

Identifying Gaps and Solutions

1. What are the hard problems that exist in AI/ML regarding acquiring and analyzing PAI?
   a. What do we need?
   b. Does that technology exist?
   c. Who is working on a solution?
2. What are some new or emerging AI/ML tools and technologies for publicly available information (PAI) analysis?
   a. Text language translations and analysis? Image/video analysis? Deepfakes? NLP? Knowledge network graphs?

Industry Landscape

1. What are the promising startups or technologies in this PAI, AI/ML space?
2. Who are the major players at the cutting edge of AI/ML for use on PAI?
   a. What makes their product/services unique?
3. Who are the relevant DoD vendors?
   a. What capabilities/platforms/data are available to purchase/acquire/replicate?

Industry and Government Collaboration

1. What is your organization's philosophy on partnering with the U.S. government? With the DoD?
2. Does your organization have an existing relationship with any military organizations or affiliates concerning PAI or AI/ML capabilities?
    a. How do you support them currently? Data? People? Computing power?
        i. Are there any challenges with the relationship?
        ii. What would make the collaboration better?
    b. If not, what is preventing the collaboration?
        i. How do you overcome that?
3. How can the Army incentivize the private sector to partner with them to leverage PAI?
4. What would a win/win look like for industry/government collaboration?
5. How can the Army reduce barriers for small firms to collaborate?

Concluding Questions

1. What's the big picture? What do you think the Army should do if they want to acquire and use PAI? What would you recommend the Army do to build up their capabilities?
2. What areas do you feel we have missed and should be considering in our work?
3. Who else would you recommend we speak to?

Protocol 2 (Industry)

General Background Questions

1. Could you please tell us a little bit about yourself to help scope the rest of the interview?
    a. What is your current position in your organization?
    b. What have been some of your past jobs?
    c. How long have you been in your current role?
2. Please describe your organizational model and products.

Current Services and Platforms

1. What data analytics, products/tools and services does your company provide?
2. What kind of data feeds into your platform?
    a. How do clients access the data used in the platform outside the platform environment?
    b. What would prohibit users from being able to access the data without use of the tool/service?
3. How do you incorporate client data into your platform?
    a. Does your platform allow for the ingestion of user-owned data?
4. Can I use your data with other programs/tools? Is there an associated cost for that capability?

Contracting

1. How do you provide these tools/services?
    a. Are the tools modular where capabilities can be added as needed to a base framework?
    b. Does your platform use a licensing structure?
        i. What does licensing look like (per seat, enterprise-wide, etc.)?
2. What is your organization's position on bundling and modularizing its capabilities?
    a. Can I use your data with other programs/tools? Is there an associated cost for that capability?
    b. Would it be advantageous to offer varying capabilities and data access levels? Why or why not?
3. What DoD entities use this service/tool/product?
    a. Geographic Combatant Commands (GCCs), Service Component Commands (SCCs), members of the Intelligence Community (IC)? Joint MISO WebOps Center (JMWC), Marine Expeditionary Forces Information Groups (MIGs), Information Warfare Center (IWC), Multi-Domain Task Force (MDTF), Information Warfare Task Force (IWTF), etc.?
    b. Who currently holds the contracts? Who authors these contracts?

Incentives

1. What kind of incentives would promote a change in how your platform or services are provided?
   a. What would the market have to be for a revamp of your business model?
   b. What are the barriers for moving to a model like that?

Miscellaneous

1. Are there any areas we should be considering concerning the rendering of services/capabilities?
2. Given our discussion today, do you have any recommendations for other organizations to talk to?

APPENDIX B

Taxonomy of Army PAI Needs

Using our SME interviews, our scenario-based workshops, and existing published joint PAI taxonomies, the RAND team developed the below taxonomy of Army PAI needs. At the top level, there are four categories of PAI needs that are essentially cyclical: sensing information, understanding information, planning operations informed by that understanding, and then assessing the effects of those operations. Within that cycle is a set of multifunctional capabilities that enable these top-level capabilities. Within each category, we identified subcategories (for example, data cleaning and data/analysis visualization). At the most granular level, we identified specific tasks within each subcategory (for example, web scraping or network visualization).

Sense

Gather and Ingest Data

- Multisource data ingest (e.g., commercial, government, SM)
- Multimedia ingest
- Modular import
- Live/real-time ingestion
- Automated ingest
- Language-agnostic ingest
- Web scraping (e.g., social and news media)
- Dark/deep web scraping
- Users-as-sensor capabilities that fuse images, content, and location data
- Remote sensing (e.g., satellite, drone, sonar data)
- Types/sources of data/media
- SM data (e.g., major English language SM, major foreign language SM [VK, WeChat], niche platforms [Telegram, Ruqqus], blogs)
- End-to-end encrypted messaging apps (e.g., WhatsApp, Signal, Telegram)
- Mass media (e.g., news application programming interfaces)
- Public records
- Localized law enforcement/crime statistics
- Local pattern-of-life data (e.g., SM platform check-ins—cell phone/mobility info)

- Logistics data, transportation/transit data
- Satellite, aerial, other overhead imagery
- Remote sensor data
- Knowledge bases/knowledge graphs
- Hospital data/public health databases
- Financial and economic databases
- Survey and polling datasets
- Geo-political databases (e.g., Armed Conflict Location and Event Data [ACLED], Global Database of Events, Language and Tone [GDELT])
- Market intelligence

Clean and Organize

Clean Data

- Clean different types of media (input missing data, add headings/labels, standardize formatting, clean ASCII strings)
- Ad stripping
- Preserved deduplication
- Error detection
- Image denoising

Index, Process, and Organize Data

- Source characterization
- Generate metadata tags
- Anonymization
- Data organization, management, hierarchy imposing, code booking, filtering
- Data enrichment
- Data normalization
- Preserve data provenance (e.g., time stamp, origin)
- Archive (to support various baselines, but also to support retrospective analysis)

Consolidate and Merge Data

- Consolidate (merge/join)
- Integration with other information sources, including intelligence and domain data
- Cross-platform linking
- Match records, assess probability of match
- Relate relevant news media, SM, and intelligence reports to one another

Understand

Explore and Describe Data

Summarize

- Summarization
- Political, Military, Economic, Social, Information, and Infrastructure (PMESII)/Areas, Structures, Capabilities, Organization, People, and Events (ASCOPE) Mapping
- Keyword identification

Media Monitoring

- News media monitoring
- News media analysis

Data Exploration or Manipulation

- Sort
- Filter
- Search
- Query (Boolean, semantic, serialized message traffic)

Detect, Identify, and Analyze Relevant Individuals and Groups

Audience, Group, or Individual Analysis

- SM listening (enriched and with analytical layers)
- Identify relevant actors and audiences
- Identify and characterize influencers
- Audience segmentation
- Characteristics and demographic detection
- Trend analysis for specific actors, audiences, or segments
- Deanonymization
- Threat analysis
- Monitor/track individuals across platforms, match records, and assess probability of match
- Track individuals' physical movements
- Pattern of life analysis/anomaly detection

Identify Coordinated Activity

- Identify inauthentic accounts
- Campaign detection
- Attributing inauthentic accounts and campaigns
- Detection of microtargeting from threat actors

Detect, Identify, and Analyze Relevant Topics

- Topic detection
- Relate sources/stream (e.g., news media, SM, intelligence reports) to one another
- Relevance scoring
- Influence scoring
- Detection, monitoring, and analysis of tensions and conflict on SM
- Analysis of tone and tension surrounding a topic
- Monitor known websites of concern

Detect Inauthentic Material

- Audiovisual forensics (e.g., detection of fake or altered video/imagery/audio)
- False or misleading information detection
- Detection of text generated by automation
- Identify data honeytraps
- Identify real-world deception (e.g., Potemkin villages or other fabricated civil society elements [virtual and physical])

Verify Authentic Material

- Fact checking
- Media authentication
- Crowd-sourced content assessments and web annotation
- Content integrity
- User account credibility assessment
- Identity verification
- Background checks of individuals, verifying or vetting (or validating, for targets)

Identify Other Concerning Activity

- Radical/extremist content detection (video, audio, text)
- Hate speech identification

Track or Monitor Content

- Monitoring, including static/mission-based, event-based, and dynamic/user-defined monitoring
- Tracking content associated with identified groups or actors of concern, including tracking the linguistic signature of a group or actor
- Tracking spread of discrete (memes, images, documents, links, hashtags, video, audio) and diffuse (topics, stories, narratives) content
- Track and analyze cross-platform content spread
- Source characterization
- Monitor topic velocity
- Operational security monitoring (e.g., signal/signature management)

- Information flow tracking, including tracking changes in internet traffic

Prediction, Indication, and Warning

- Detection and alerts of emergent or concerning events and threats in the information environment
- Thresholding (how much of a predictive signal is enough to flag for human attention)
- Timely/real-time alerts (rather than post-hoc or delayed analysis)
- Structured and secure tactics, techniques, and procedures/event reporting and sharing, comparable with Structured Threat Information eXpression (STIX)/Trusted Automated eXchange of Intelligence Information (TAXII) for cyber
- Predictive analytics and forecasting
- Predict potential for virality
- Risk/threat assessment

Plan Operations

- Analytical tasks included elsewhere are also relevant here
- Standard military planning tasks
- Digital IE sandbox

Assess Courses of Action and Plans

- Analytical tasks included elsewhere are also relevant here
- Standard military assessment tasks
- Monitoring response to stimulus (e.g., changes because of U.S. presence/operations, changes because of adversary presence/operations)
- Engagement assessment
- Messaging effectiveness measurement (e.g., resonance analysis)
- Receipt confirmation
- Understand and track opinion formation across platforms
- Measure of performance/measure of effort mapping

Multifunctional Capabilities

Visualization

- Geo-spatial location of events and actors, where appropriate
- Timeline
- Knowledge graphs

- Network visualizations, including social network mapping and relationship maps (at different levels, e.g., individual, community, meta-community)
- Information environment visualizations/overlays
- Data visualization
- Embedded language translation
- Common operating picture
- Trend visualization
- Topic visualization
- User visualization configuration

Narrative and Discourse Analyses

- Narrative analysis
- Narrative identification
- Counternarrative suggestions
- Conversation analysis
- Political advertising analysis
- Motivation detection
- Behavior, sentiment, stance, and bias analysis

Network Analysis

- Network analysis
- Network intelligence
- Large-scale network tracking
- Link analysis
- Identify network centrality and use patterns by group
- Characterize uncertainty among key ties in networks
- Identify key network entry points and information pathways

Natural Language Processing

- Scraping/encoding/loading text data
- Parsing/tokenizing/tagging text data
- Text pre-processing
- Entity enrichment
- Text segmentation
- Document processing/cleaning
- Training data generation
- Inductive text analysis/corpus methods
- Text/document similarity
- Natural language understanding

- Natural language generation
- Interactive NLP applications
- Speech recognition
- Entity resolution (e.g., linking a real-world entity [phone number, credit score] to a digital record)

Machine Learning Estimators (Entities, Images, Video, Memes, Documents, Audio, etc.)

- Classification
- Clustering
- Regression
- Dimensionality reduction

Geographic Information Systems

- Geo-inferencing
- Spatial overlays
- Sociocultural overlays
- Boundary analysis

Vision and Biometrics

- Biometrics for identity authentication
- Object detection
- Speech detection/audio fingerprinting
- Face detection/recognition
- Machine vision (e.g., object and entity recognition in imagery and video)

Machine Translation

- Automated speech recognition/transcription
- Machine translation

Social Science Foundation and Modeling

- Understanding drivers of behavior
- Predictive social science modeling

Information Capability Area Needs

Our scenario-based analysis helped us better understand the Army's needs for the various PAI capabilities and activities in our taxonomy. We then crosswalked those needs within PAI subcategories against the various informational capability areas across the Army. Figures C.1, C.2, C.3, and C.4 provide visualizations of PAI needs across the IRCs.

FIGURE C.1

Information Capabilities Area: Sense Requirements

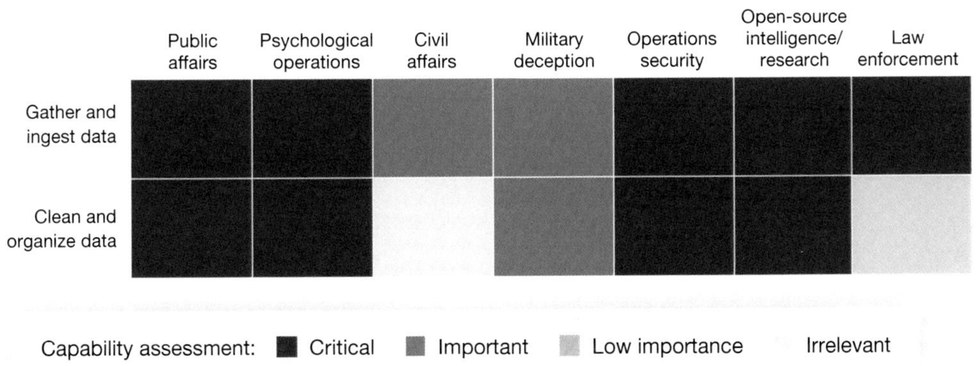

FIGURE C.2

Information Capabilities Area: Understand Requirements

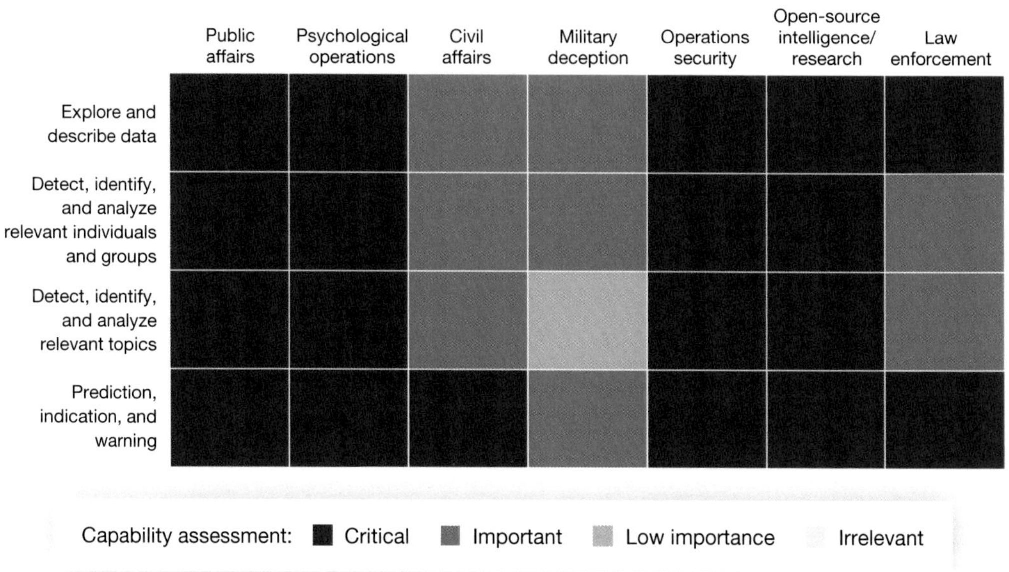

FIGURE C.3

Information Capabilities Area: Plan and Assess Requirements

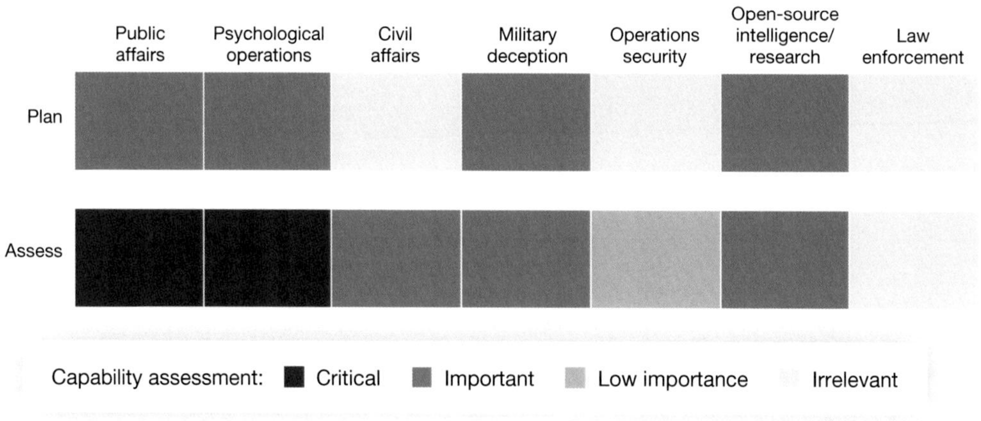

FIGURE C.4

Information Capabilities Area: Multifunctional Capabilities Requirements

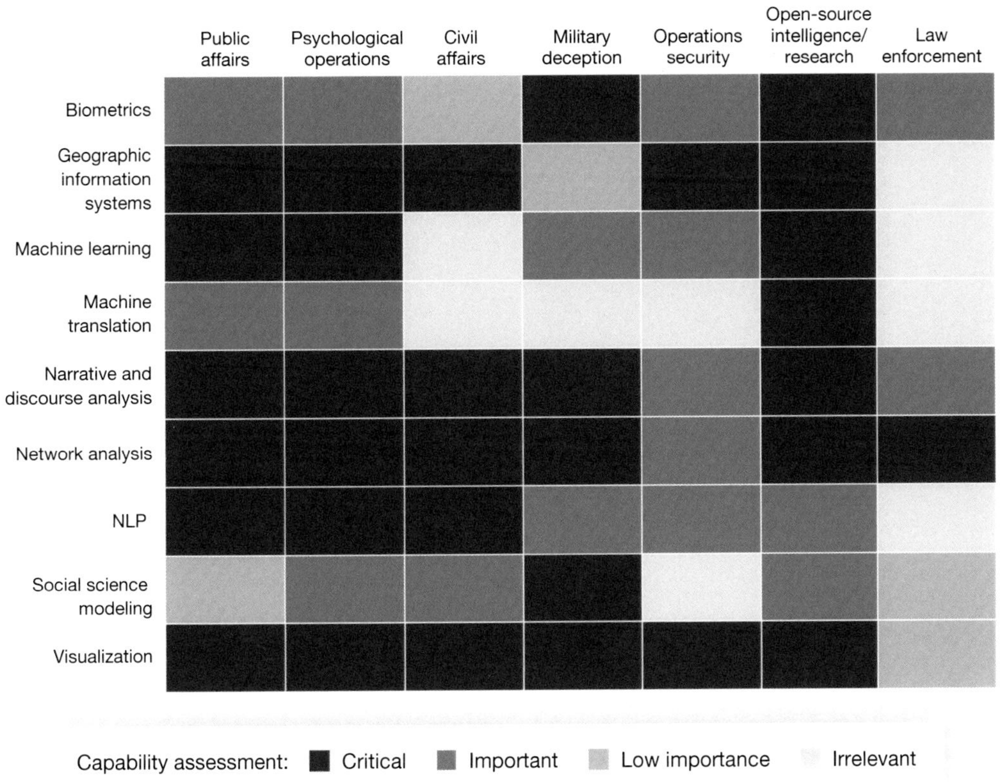

APPENDIX D

Scenarios

Scenario-Based Analyses and Workshops

We conducted a series of scenario-based capabilities analyses to further elicit potential requirements for a robust, relevant PAI analytic capability across the Army. These scenarios were short, fictional vignettes covering different situations in which PAI and various information capability areas (e.g., PA, law enforcement, operations security, open-source intelligence, military deception, CA, and MISO) could be utilized. The five scenarios that we explored were (1) viral Army stories, (2) force protection, (3) early warning, (4) stability operations, and (5) regime change. Transcriptions of the worksheets from each session are included in the following sections.

Scenario 1: Detection of Army-Relevant Stories

Over the course of the year, 13 soldiers have gone missing or been found dead from Fort H—, a large installation housing an infantry division. The most notorious case, with the greatest media and public attention, has been for a soldier who was brutally murdered by a fellow soldier after being missing for almost a year. After initially denying that the murdered soldier had reported sexual harassment prior to her disappearance, the Army revealed that she had twice reported harassment to her chain of command. Additionally, the soldier accused of her murder was still on active duty while being investigated for sexual assault, and, after the discovery of remains, killed himself. This incident has focused media attention on Fort H—, with media cataloguing and detailing missing and dead soldiers from the base. In this scenario, an ability to analyze social and digital news media sources is critical to supporting informational capabilities.

Timeline

The timeline of this scenario progressed over the course of 71 weeks.

- Week 1: Stories begin to circulate over SM raising awareness of the missing soldier.

- Week 2: U.S. media outlets begin to cover story. In interviews, family claims the soldier had been sexually harassed by other soldiers and that her unit leadership had failed their daughter.
- Week 3: Fort H—'s PA office (PAO) issues statements about the missing soldier (under absent without leave [AWOL] status), including denial that the soldier had been the victim of sexual harassment.
  - Social and traditional media attention increases. The Office of the Chief of PA (OCPA) issues a statement that the Army will conduct an investigation.
- Weeks 4–9: Social and traditional media criticism of the Army continues. Additional soldier missing/killed cases are brought to light. OCPA continues to message about the U.S. Army's commitment to soldiers and preventing sexual harassment/assault. **The volume of stories, the specific outlets, and the types of accounts involved indicate that foreign adversaries are boosting this narrative as part of a malign information effort meant to degrade U.S. Army operational capabilities.**
- Weeks 10–49: Social and traditional media criticism of the Army continues. Additional soldier missing/killed cases are brought to light. This case becomes a touchstone/exemplar of why the U.S. military cannot be trusted to investigate sexual assault and is brought up for all sexual assault/harassment stories, including for other services. OCPA continues to message about the U.S. Army's commitment to soldiers and preventing sexual harassment/assault. **The volume of apparently foreign malign informational efforts continues to rise through week 15.**
- Week 50: The remains of the missing soldier are discovered. The suspect in the missing soldier's disappearance, who had been under unarmed guard (under pretense of violating coronavirus disease 2019 restrictions) escapes custody, is confronted by local law enforcement, and shoots himself. **Apparently, foreign malign information efforts on this narrative decline, but the narrative's velocity and effects seem to be self-sustaining.**
- Week 51: The parents of the dead soldier accuse the Army and local police of executing the suspect as part of a cover-up.
- Week 60: OCPA apologizes on behalf of the Army for listing the murdered soldier as AWOL and announces a new policy requiring that ambiguous missing soldier cases be labeled as such.
- Week 71: The Secretary of Defense announces that U.S. military commanders will no longer have authority to investigate or prosecute sexual assault cases and establishes an independent review commission of highly qualified experts to oversee all military sexual assault cases. Sexual assault is added to the Uniform Code of Military Justice as an offense.

PA Office Functions

The following responsibilities would fall to the PA office.

- *Advise and counsel*: At all echelons, public affairs officers are the primary staff officers serving as the principal public communication adviser to the commander on all PA matters. Public affairs officers possess review and release authority for all information and products intended for the public, lead the commander's communication synchronization process, coordinate with sister information capabilities, and ensure that command-level communication initiatives align.
- *Media relations*: PAOs help the public understand the military by facilitating engagement between national and international media outlets and soldiers, escorting media throughout operational and training environments, and creating news and information products that inform the public on Army activities at home and abroad.
- *Community outreach*: PAOs facilitate engagement with local communities and fulfill the commander's requirement to inform the American people and all stakeholders of Army activities and initiatives.
- *Command information*: PAOs are responsible for a large portion of internal command messaging. Audiences include the command, soldiers, subordinate leaders, and Army families.
- *Digital media management*: PAOs use a variety of aligned digital communication tools to instantaneously tell the Army's story, stay connected with the Army family and share Army information accurately and in a timely manner.
- *Deterring adversaries and countering propaganda*: In tactical and operational environments, and when appropriate, PAOs synchronize and coordinate with the information operations working group. It is important to note that PA and Information Operations both directly support military objectives, but their activities differ with respect to intent, scope, and audience and are governed by separate procedures. All information dissemination, regardless of the communicator or medium, is intended to either inform or influence. It is important to note that commanders use non–PA information activities to communicate to select, non-American publics to change or maintain attitudes, beliefs, and behaviors.

Scenario 2: Early Warning for Threats to the Force

A mass shooting incident at Ft. R— has left the Army community stunned: An active shooter targeted families in base housing, killing 12 dependents and two soldiers before being shot and killed by military police (MP). The three families targeted were Asian-American and Latinx. Subsequent to the shooting, evidence emerged that the shooter was affiliated with racially and ethnically motivated violent extremist (REMVE) groups. The shooter, SPC S—, had posted increasingly angry and disaffected SM posts over the course of the past year, before deleting public SM accounts the week before the shooting. He had numerous disciplinary issues and had received two separate Article 15s over the past year. One of those citations had resulted in a demotion in rank from SGT to SPC. In this scenario, an ability to analyze individual social and media accounts is critical to supporting informational capabilities.

Timeline

The timeline of this scenario progressed over the course of 31 weeks.

- Week 1: SPC S— (formerly SGT S—) begins to post to his main SM account complaining about his demotion in rank. He blames his leadership and a culture that victimizes white men as political scapegoats for social problems and says negative things about the Army and how he has been treated after deploying.
- Weeks 2–10: SPC S—'s SM feed becomes increasingly political, talking about and linking to increasingly fringe discourses and conspiracy theories. Prior to his demotion in rank, SPC S—'s feed mostly consisted of pictures of his family/children and stories about his favorite baseball teams. He also begins to frequent message boards and sites for conspiracy theories.
- Week 11: SPC S— joins several public websites and a public messaging app channel that feature REMVE content and that urge members to prepare for violent ethnic conflict and the end of the United States. His pseudonyms on these sites are variations of "Lars Sørensen," lead singer of a Norwegian metal band, Helsdottir, that is associated with anti-immigrant violence in Nordic European countries. His persona on two of these sites includes a profile picture of him in mission-oriented protective posture gear, pointing his carbine at the camera.
- Weeks 12–17: SPC S—'s SM feed is now solely fringe conservative and conspiracy discourses, including an increasing amount of anti-immigrant, anti-Islamic, and coded racist content.
- Weeks 18–22: SPC S— posts less frequently on his public SM account. He starts using an anonymous browser, finds extremist content on the deep web, and makes contact with the REMVE group The Patriot Alliance, a group known to recruit active and former military members.
- Weeks 23–25: SPC S— begins to post on his public SM feed again, but it is almost exclusively racist and anti-immigrant memes. Much of the content posted to his public page is also posted, around the same time, on his "Lars Sørenson" accounts.
- Week 26: SPC S—'s command begins an administrative separation process against him.
- Week 30: SPC S— posts pictures of his children with messages of his love for them.
  - At 1800, SPC S— goes to the post housing for E-5-and-below soldiers and begins to open fire on family members on X— Street, moving up the street and skipping two homes that house families of European descent. Fort R— MP members respond quickly, and a firefight and standoff occurs, with one MP seriously wounded. Other MPs are able to take up firing positions from behind where SPC S— has taken cover and kill him.
- Week 31: The subsequent investigation shows that, while SPC S— was legally allowed to possess both a hunting rifle and a 9mm pistol in his on-post housing, he had amassed a large collection of semi-automatic weapons, pyrotechnic devices, and explosive ordnance (C-4 and detonation cord) that appeared to be stolen military property.

Scenario 3: Threat Warning of Impending Conflict

Tensions have been increasing between Krasnovia and neighboring Pinelandia over what each side calls provocation in the region. Throughout the 20th century, Krasnovia and Pinelandia have fought several actions over this region, the most recent of which was in the 1990s. Increasingly there are internal calls from Krasnovian media and public figures to take action to "defend ethnic Krasnovians and Krasnovia's historic borders," by implication meaning annexing western Pinelandia. There are many ethnic Krasnovians and Krasnov speakers in the western region, and there is a narrative in Krasnovia around "territorial integrity" that would include this area. Reports have emerged that Krasnovian troops are mobilizing near the border, and there are reports of "little gray men" filtering into western Pinelandia. Strangely, internet connectivity has been spotty in western Pinelandia over the past week, and some areas have been completely blacked out. In this scenario, an ability to analyze commercial satellite imagery, transportation and logistics information, and SM sources is critical to supporting informational capabilities.

Timeline

The timeline of this scenario progressed over the course of nine weeks.

- Week 1: Krasnovian forces conduct *Kraspad*-202X, an annual six-day strategic military exercise that rotates through four operating areas in Krasnovia.
- Week 2: After *Kraspad*-202X, Krasnovian special forces units remain in the area, not far from the Pinelandia border to the east. The western area of Ponblass was formerly occupied by Krasnovia in the 20th century, and there is a majority of ethnic Krasnovians in the area.
- Week 3: Elite Krasnovian Special Operations Command (*Krasnatz*-SOC) teams begin to cross into Pinelandia. They are dressed in civilian clothes and carry cell phones and personal weapons. They take up commercial lodgings near the airport, power plants, television and radio stations, transit hubs, and bridges along main supply routes (MSRs) into the western region of Pinelandia. While the SOC teams are conducting reconnaissance on infrastructure and bridges, local citizens photograph two different Krasnovian teams, speculating on who the men are. While some Pinelandians use the English language *FaceSpace* platform, these photographs are posted to popular Krasnovian-language platform *PK*.
- Weeks 4–5: Personnel and equipment from the Krasnovian 99th Combined Guards Brigade (BDE) begin to flow to the border region. Company-sized units of soldiers move by way of passenger rail and then are transported by bus to barracks staging areas at a base only 18 km from the border. Logistics vehicles, infantry fighting vehicles, armored personnel carriers, self-propelled artillery, self-propelled missile systems, and two companies of armor are all moved via commercial rail and then staged at vehicle and tank parks on the base with overhead camouflage-netting cover. Several times during this troop movement, Krasnovian soldiers take selfies and post them to *PK* and *FaceSpace*.

The vast majority of these pictures are posted with geo-tagging off, but two pictures of soldiers that include identifiable equipment with unit designations in the background are posted with geo-tagging on.

- Week 6: *Krasnatz*-SF (special forces) units begin crossing the border into Pinelandia in platoon-size units. They carry personal weapons and communications gear and wear standard Krasnovian digital camouflage pattern field uniforms stripped of insignia or rank. They use local commuter trolleys and buses, and multiple squads of *Krasnatz*-SF forces are photographed or filmed and posted to SM platforms, mostly to *PK* but also to *FaceSpace*. One particularly clear video of members on a bus goes viral, with ethnic Krasnovian veterans correctly identifying service rifles, a light machine gun, and a sniper rifle all currently issued to Krasnovian forces. At the end of the week, memes about little gray men circulate on *FaceSpace*.
- Week 7: *Krasnatz*-SF make contact with local "self-defense" (separatist) militias, and several pictures are circulated that show *Krasnatz* forces training militia forces in open spaces, such as parks.
- Week 8: Krasnovian military forces seize Ponblass:
  - An internet blackout turns off all internet access in the greater Ponblass region.
  - Units from the 99th Combined Guards BDE flow across the border at three different locations.
  - *Krasnatz*-SF, with very minimal help from militia members, seize the local Pinelandian Defense Force (PDF) garrison after a brief engagement.
  - *Krasnatz*-SOC teams also seize critical infrastructure and demolish bridges on and adjacent to MSRs that connect to parts of Pinelandia, blocking ground access for PDF units from the country's interior.
  - There is a coordinated SM campaign from the Krasnovian government, Krasnovian media (controlled by the government), and *Krasnov Adepts* (nominally independent political commentators who are in fact tools of the state) portraying the action in Ponblass as peacekeeping—local militias stopped the PDF from attacking local citizens, and Krasnovia sent in a small force to stabilize and bring peace to the region. Ethnic Krasnov political leaders in Ponblass support this influence campaign. SM is filled with photos and videos—all doctored, deepfakes, or decontextualized from other conflicts—that purport to show PDF atrocities.
- Week 9: The internet in the greater Ponblass region is restored. Krasonvian forces occupy all major television and radio stations, critical infrastructure, and transit hubs. PDF forces that attempt to move into the areas of responsibility via alternate routes are blocked by elements of the 99th Combined Guards BDE. Krasnovia has effectively presented Pinelandia and the world with a *fait accompli*.

Scenario 4: Civilian-Military Interaction in Stability Operations

Elements of the 101st Airborne are deployed to Northern Ariana to help stabilize the region after the Islamic State of Iraq and Syria (ISIS) forces have run rampant over much of the area for years. While U.S. Special Operations Forces (SOF) helped train and equip ethnic minority Turgistani forces to combat ISIS, the mission has transitioned to one of stabilization. CA forces have arrived and are helping rebuild infrastructure, restore civilian governance, relocate displaced civilians, and support local police forces running a prison containing both ISIS fighters and suspected families of ISIS fighters. Turgistanis (who are Sunni) make up the majority of the locals. However, there are some local Shia from the ethnic majority of the populace in the rest of the country. There is a lot of tension between these two groups and between the region and the rest of the country. Various clerics and political leaders have different opinions about national unity and governance in the region.

Elements from each group are active on SM and there is a local government-funded radio station that broadcasts to the area. Some locals own personal computers and there are a few internet cafes in the region, but the vast majority of SM and communications is from mobile devices (78 percent of internet communications are via mobile device). Android users are the vast majority (86 percent) over Apple devices, and the two dominant SM platforms are Facebook/Facebook Messenger and Snapchat.

The theater campaign plan outlines the following six lines of effort (LOEs) for the region:

1. establishment of a single, transparent, market-based economy fully integrated with the remainder of Ariana and its neighbors
2. establishment of democratic institutions and the conduct of elections that result in representation of the diverse population of Northern Ariana
3. establishment of the rule of law that fosters the confidence of the people in the legal and judicial systems
4. establishment of a national identity among the citizens of Northern Ariana that results in a shared view of themselves as belonging to Ariana
5. the repair of infrastructure to the extent that basic life services are restored and improved to international standards and natural resources are used to allow for the equitable economic development of all Arianis
6. establishment of professional border security forces and military forces to international standards and basing of Arianian military forces answerable to civilian leadership.

An important set of supporting tasks for LOE 2 is to

- establish a time-phased plan to conduct the first general election
- conduct a census to facilitate voter registration
- support enforcement of new election laws that establish national standards to formalize election procedures

- prevent religious/ethnic disenfranchisement
- establish provisional election commission
- develop the local capacity to administer elections
- establish and enforce voter residency requirements
- provide international monitoring of elections
- assist with the implementation of election results.

An important set of supporting tasks for LOE 5 is to

- develop an infrastructure priorities list that reflects the most urgent regional and local needs, with an eye to both immediate needs, such as utility and road services, and to long-term well-being and economic growth
- oversee the creation of a regional board and local boards to confer and consult with U.S. forces on fair and equitable distribution of infrastructure funds
- ensure that infrastructure funds and activities are fair and equitable, aligning with outcomes for LOE 4
- oversee the creation of a fair and transparent bidding system for local contracting and labor forces
- produce population and economic overlay maps for the region
- produce socially meaningful road-use overlay maps for the region.

In this scenario, an ability to analyze publicly available geospatial data, government databases, and social and digital news media sources is critical to supporting informational capabilities.

Scenario 5: Pro-Reform MISO Campaign

Since disputed elections in 2018, Atropia has been a divided country. The current regime, a dictatorship under President Raja Murad, has become increasingly unpopular: More than 4 million Atropians have left the country as refugees since the election, and the economy is in freefall with rolling blackouts and a severe devaluation of the currency. Hyperinflation has made the most basic goods extremely expensive, and medicine and medical care are reserved for only the elite class and the military.

The United States supports the opposition Atropia Workers Party (PWK) and its jailed leader, Tariq Uzair, while both Krasnovia and Tianxīn publicly support the regime. Krasnovia is providing direct military aid to Atropia, while the United States has led economic sanction efforts against the Murad regime, accusing Atropia of supporting and exporting terrorism. U.S. SOF are stationed across the border in Qumaria conducting partner and assist missions with displaced PWK forces who hope to go back to Atropia as part of a popular uprising. In support of this, U.S. Army Central is conducting MISO efforts meant to influence multiple audiences in Atropia, in the region, and globally. In this scenario, an ability to analyze social and digital news media sources is critical to supporting informational capabilities.

MISO Planning

Potential audiences include

- individuals within the Murad regime who might be turned against him, particularly the Atropia military
- global and regional influencers on SM
- Atropia's civilian populace
- Qumarian (neighbor) populace and government
- regional U.S. partners

Campaign goals include

- increasing resistance inside Atropia to the Murad regime
- legitimizing PWK in the eyes of the region/globe
- shaming Krasnovia and Tianxīn globally as supporting human rights violations by the Murad regime
- framing U.S. involvement so that it is not seen as a threat by regional partners with authoritarian-leaning governments.

APPENDIX E

Data Taxonomy

This appendix provides a broad overview of the categories of PAI data that can be acquired and the types of sources from which such data might be acquired. It is not intended to be comprehensive—there are additional categories of data available in the public sphere that we did not include in this taxonomy. Instead, this appendix is intended to give the reader a flavor of the scope and diversity of data available in the public domain and the types of sources that catalog these data.

We created this taxonomy by exploring several different types of data sources. First, we reviewed the digital advertising platforms made available by Alphabet (Google) and Meta (Facebook) to understand what data characteristics they made available for targeted advertising. Additionally, we reviewed the types of data made available by businesses that aggregate data and make it available for purchase (*data brokers*). Acxiom provided us with their data catalog, and we also reviewed the categories on *Datarade*, a website that helps businesses identify which data broker has the type of data they might want to purchase. Finally, we reviewed data provided by government agencies, such as the National Aeronautics and Space Administration (NASA), National Oceanic and Atmospheric Administration (NOAA), and United States Geological Survey (USGS). We then constructed the data taxonomy shown in Tables E.1 and E.2 to capture the major categories of publicly available data and illustrate some of the disparate sources that could potentially provide that type of data.

TABLE E.1
Individually Identified Data

Category	Example Sources	Definition
Demographic Data		
Occupation and Employment Data		
Wage/Income History Data	Data brokers, digital advertising platforms	The payment an individual has received in compensation for their work
Employment History Data	SM, job search/ employment websites	The jobs an individual has held over their career
Education Data		
Grade Level/Terminal Degree Data	Data brokers, SM, job search websites	The highest level of education an individual has received

Table E.1—Continued

Category	Example Sources	Definition
Identity Data		
Ethnic Affiliation Data	Data brokers, digital advertising platforms	The ethnicity or ethnicities with which an individual identifies
Religious Affiliation Data	Data brokers, SM, digital advertising platforms	The religious or spiritual beliefs to which an individual adheres or religious/ spiritual groups to which an individual belongs
Lifestyle Preferences	Data brokers, digital advertising platforms, SM	This can include habits, interests, hobbies, political affiliations, and attitudes
Household Data		
Place of Residence Data	Data brokers, voter registration databases, Department of Motor Vehicles (DMV) records	Where an individual typically lives, eats, and sleeps
Partnership Status Data	Data brokers, digital advertising platforms, local government records	Marital/cohabitation status
Family Unit Data	Data brokers, digital advertising platforms	Number of children, the ages of any children, demographics about other close family members or household members
Personally Identifiable Information Data		
Age Data	Data brokers, digital advertising platforms, local government	How old the individual is, their date of birth
Life Events Data	Data brokers, digital advertising platforms, SM	Getting engaged/married, buying a house, having children, getting promoted at work, etc.
Life Stage Data	Data brokers, digital advertising platforms, SM	A combination of environmental factors shaping an individual's interests, tastes, etc. Most commonly influenced by age, life events, and career stage
Government Personally Identifiable Information Data		
Government Identifiers and Documentation	State, local, and federal government	Social Security number, Green card/ alien registration, driver's license, passport, etc.

Table E.1—Continued

Category	Example Sources	Definition
Goods Data		
Car Ownership Data		
Car Details Data	Data brokers, digital advertising platforms, DMV	For example, the car's make, model, and age
Own/Lease Data	Data brokers, digital advertising platforms, DMV	Whether the individual owns or leases their car(s), years left on the lease/car loan
Technology Ownership Data		
Mobile Device Data	Data brokers, digital advertising platforms	Whether the individual owns any mobile phone or other mobile device as well as technical details about the device (operating system, age, whether it can display video ads, etc.)
Television Data	Data brokers, digital advertising platforms	Whether the individual owns a television, the brand and model, how content is delivered, etc.
Lifestyle and Behavior Data		
Behavior Data		
Interests and Activities Data	Data brokers, digital advertising platforms, SM	Wide range of interests and activities—interested in/play sports, interest in various news topics, whether they attend religious services, etc.
Intent Data	Data brokers, digital advertising platforms, SM	Whether the behavior of an individual indicates that that person might be about to do something—buy a car, move their place of residence, change jobs, etc.
Sentiment Data	Data brokers, digital advertising platforms, SM	How an individual feels about brands, products, organizations, etc.
Health Care Data		
Biometric Data	Data brokers	Records about an individual's current health status (collected from medical tests [physicals, eye exams, etc.], wearable devices, or other sources); typically available only at an aggregate or anonymized level
Medical Records Data	Data brokers	Anonymized, patient-level datasets typically used for medical research
Genomic Data	Data brokers, genealogy websites	The genome and DNA data of organisms, used in bioinformatics

Table E.1—Continued

Category	Example Sources	Definition
Personal Financial Data		
Net Worth Data	Data brokers, digital advertising platforms	The total net worth of an individual
Income Data	Data brokers, digital advertising platforms	The current income and income history of an individual
Loans Data	Data brokers, credit rating companies	How much an individual owes in different types of loan instruments (car loan, mortgage, etc.)
Credit Rating Data	Data brokers, credit rating companies	The assessed credit rating for an individual
Friends/Social Circle Data		
Number of Connections	SM, data brokers, digital advertising platforms	Primarily derived from SM, but could also be calculated from other sources (such as phone calls or text messages)
Influence Level	SM, data brokers, digital advertising platforms	Measures how impactful this individual's opinion is on others
Frequency of Interaction/ Communication	SM, data brokers, digital advertising platforms	Number of contacts per day/week
Current/Former Expat	SM, data brokers, digital advertising platforms	Whether this individual has ever lived abroad (or in a specific country)
Has Friends Living Abroad	SM, data brokers, digital advertising platforms	Whether this individual has any friends/ contacts living abroad (or in a specific country)

TABLE E.2

Nationally Identified Data

Category	Example Sources	Definition
Geospatial Data		
Places Data		
Business Location data	State government, data brokers, open-source GIS databases	Where a business is located, what kind of business it is, the name/brand associated with the location, business category, etc. Specific business types can be specified—fueling stations, restaurants, warehouses, etc.
Point of Interest data	Data brokers, open-source GIS databases	Information about real-world public places, such as businesses, government facilities, parks, monuments, and other sites of convenience or tourist attractions
Architectural/Structures Data		
Building Footprint Data	Data brokers, open-source GIS databases	A polygon, or set of polygons, representing a specific building in the physical world
Property Transaction Data	Data brokers, local governments, real estate databases	Information about the purchase and sale of items of property in real estate
Property Owner Data	Data brokers, local governments	A person or organization with the legal right and ability to create, alter, share, or restrict any piece or set of data
Map Data		
Satellite Imagery Data	NASA, NOAA, USGS, Google Earth, data brokers	Remotely sensed satellite data. Typically grouped into two basic types: passively collected data and actively collected data.
GIS Data	NGA, NASA, data brokers	Contains a variety of geographically referenced information. This can include the latitude/longitude of the location, the location's elevation, soil conditions, and other environmental factors.
Cellular Data		
Cell Tower Data	Telecommunications, Data brokers	The location of the cell tower, the number of people connected to it, how much data they are using, the calls routed through the tower, etc.
Network Data	Internet Service Providers, Data brokers	The type of network used to connect to phone networks or the internet. These can include such technologies as 3G, 4G, 5G, LAN, or WAN.

Table E.2—Continued

Category	Example Sources	Definition
Pattern of Life Data		
Foot Traffic Data	Data brokers	The number of customers who enter a location and patterns of activity—often a business but this can also include government facilities or public places
Trip Data	Data brokers	Deidentified and aggregated data elements related to trips taken by users of a shared mobility device, including Global Positioning System, time stamp, or route data
Visit Data	Data brokers	Data collected from a specific interaction with a customer/visitor. Often these details are required as part of the delivery of a service—contact information, purpose of visit, etc.
Logistics Data		
Traffic Data		
Rail Traffic Data	Federal Railroad Administration, data brokers	Includes volume of rail traffic, types of railcars, specific routes traveled, etc.
Trucking Traffic Data	Department of Transportation, data brokers	Trucking traffic data includes volume counts, vehicle classification counts, and speed data.
Car Traffic Data	Department of Transportation, data brokers	Car traffic data consists of time stamped geolocation data that indicate the speeds and directions at which vehicles are moving on a particular roadway or area.
Ride-Sharing Data	Data brokers	Information about the aggregate number of drivers who work for ride-share companies as well as passengers who use these services.
Marine Traffic Data	Coast Guard, data brokers	Location of maritime vessels, their expected routes, and characteristics of the vessels.
Air Traffic Data	FAA, data brokers, FlightAware	Aviation data contains traffic information on public flights, air traffic control, and air cargo routes.
Freight Data		
Good Values and Volume Data	Data brokers	The commodity categories' price according to types and amount by state or country.

Table E.2—Continued

Category	Example Sources	Definition
Commodity Attributes Data	Data brokers	The types of commodities sent and the legal restrictions on these goods.
Weight Attributes Data	Data brokers	The total weight of the shipment.
Trade Data		
Import/Export Data	Data brokers	The import and export of data on the automated or semi-automated input and output of datasets between different software applications.
Global Trade Data	Data brokers	Import and export statistics, typically organized by time period, country, and commodity.
Shipment Data	Data brokers	The qualities of the cargo and transport moving it.
Road Data		
Trucking Fleet Data	Department of Transportation	Includes such information as where vehicles are, what assets a company has on hand, and the safety record of drivers and vehicles.
Road Condition Data	Bureau of Transportation Statistics	The conditions of the surface roads as they are reported in real time.
Rail Data		
Rail Geographic System Data	Federal Railroad Administration	The conditions of railroad tracks and other railroad infrastructure.
Grade Crossing Data	Federal Railroad Administration	Includes such data as accident and safety data, the effect on travel time, and the effect on auto emission reductions.
Marine Shipping Data		
U.S. Vessel Movement and Port Calls Data	Department of Transportation	Port calls at U.S. ports categorized by vessel type and capacity.
Vessel Fleet Lists Data	Department of Transportation	Information about the numbers, types, and characteristics of merchant vessels worldwide.
Aviation Data		
Aircraft Data	FAA	The vital information about an aircraft, such as its age, fuel capacity, and other details.

Table E.2—Continued

Category	Example Sources	Definition
Air Control Data	FAA	The movement of aircraft within and between airports by receiving and processing data from radar and devices that monitor local weather conditions and by maintaining radio contact with pilots.
Environmental Data		
Weather Data	NOAA	Data used to track weather patterns and predict trends. Can include such indicators as minimum/maximum temperature, humidity, or wind speed.
Climate Data	EPA	Measured parameters that help specify the climate of a specific location or region, such as precipitation, temperature, wind speed, and humidity.
Air Quality Index Data	EPA	A measure of how clean or polluted air is, and what the associated health effects might be.
Wildfires Data	U.S. Forest Service	Pre-event and post-fire event imagery. This can be used to assess smoke and ash transport, burn severity, vegetation loss, and more.
Marine Data	NOAA	There are four general categories of marine data collection: marine scientific research, surveys, operational oceanography, and exploration and exploitation.
Water Data	USGS	Quantifies the availability of water resources. Also provides details about the flow of groundwater and measures the impacts of abstraction.
Land Use Data	U.S. Department of Agriculture	How people utilize land—whether for agricultural, recreational, residential, commercial, or industrial purposes.
Geological Data	USGS	Data and information gathered through or derived from geological and geochemical techniques.
Surface Data	NOAA	Meteorological data that are measured at the earth's surface (technically, somewhere between ground level and 10m).
Atmosphere Data	NOAA	Environmental information that is related to how the weather at atmosphere is at some point in time.

Table E.2—Continued

Category	Example Sources	Definition
Ionospheric Data	NOAA	Information about the ionosphere's recorded behavior and solar activity.
Thermosphere Data	NOAA	Environmental information that is related to the thermosphere, the fourth layer of the earth's atmosphere that absorbs the sun's radiation.
Geodemographic Data	Data brokers	Location-based data that segments individuals based on where they live and their demographic profile.
Legal and Regulatory Data		
Intellectual Property Data	World Intellectual Property Organization	Includes records of patents, trademarks, copyrights, etc.
Bankruptcy Data	State governments, data brokers	Details about the legal status of a company as a result of its declared bankruptcy.
Litigation Data	State governments, data brokers	Details about pending litigation.
Crime Data	State, local, and federal governments, data brokers	Statistics about the types and locations of reported crimes.
Informatics		
Clickstream Data		
Real-Time and Historical Click Frequency Data	Data brokers	Details about how and how often users are interacting with a website.
User Journey Data	Data brokers	Data showing how a user progressed from an initial search or landing page to buying an item or service.
Aggregated Click Frequency Data	Data brokers	Aggregate data about which pages a website visitor visits and in what order.
IP Address Data		
IP to Geolocation Data	Internet Service Providers, data brokers	The mapping of IP addresses of internet-connected devices to their geographic location in the real world.
Mobile IP Data	Internet Service Providers, data brokers	Links IP addresses with their mobile carriers. Often used for customer profiling or cybersecurity.
Company IP Data	Internet Service Providers, data brokers	Links IP addresses with a company or organization.

Table E.2—Continued

Category	Example Sources	Definition
Anonymous IP Data	Internet Service Providers, data brokers	Profiles the use of anonymous IP addresses.
Web Search Data		
Online Search Trends Data	Internet Service Providers, data brokers	How often specific keywords, subjects, and phrases have been queried over a specific period of time.
Search Engine Optimization Data	Internet Service Providers, data brokers	*Search engine optimization* (the process used to optimize a website's technical configuration, content relevance, and link popularity so its pages can become easily findable, more relevant, and popular toward user search queries, which leads to higher search engine ranking).
Search Engine Results Page Data	Internet Service Providers, data brokers	*Search engine results page* is the page that a search engine returns after a user submits a search query.
Web Activity Data	Internet Service Providers, data brokers	The record of human actions in the online or physical world that can be captured by computer.
News Data	Internet Service Providers, data brokers	Information regarding current events, recent events, newsworthy events, and current affairs likely to be of interest to a broadcaster's target listeners in the markets.
Web Scraping Data	Data brokers	Data gathered from websites.
Internet of Things Data		
Status Data	Data brokers	Basic, raw data that communicate the status of a device or system.
Automation Data	Data brokers	Data created by automated devices and such systems as smart thermostats and automated lighting.
Orientation Data	Data brokers	The geographic location of a device or system. These data are frequently used in logistics, warehousing, and manufacturing.
Economic Data		
Transaction Data		
Credit Card Transaction Data	Data brokers	Financial data generally collected through the transfer of funds between a cardholder's account and a business's account.

Table E.2—Continued

Category	Example Sources	Definition
Debit Card Transaction Data	Data brokers	Financial data generally collected through the transfer of funds between a cardholder's account and a business's account.
Sales Transaction Data	Data brokers	Transaction information collected by a company in connection with sale of goods, including the amount of the sale, a description of the items sold, the date and location of such sale, and loyalty program information.
Bank Transaction Data	Data brokers	Information that is captured from transactions. It records the time of the transaction, the place where it occurred, the price points, etc.
Business-to-Business Transaction Data	Data brokers	Records describing the time of the transaction, the place where it occurred, the price points of the items bought, the payment method employed, discounts, if any, and other quantities and qualities associated with the transaction.
Consumer Transaction Data		
Point-of-Sale Transaction Data	Data brokers	A payment for goods or services, usually made in a retail setting. Point-of-sale transactions can be conducted in person or online
Industrial Transaction Data	Data brokers	Records describing the time of the transaction, the place where it occurred, the price points of the items bought, the payment method employed, discounts, if any, and other quantities and qualities associated with the transaction.
Tickerized Transaction Data	Data brokers	Aggregate metrics, such as total number of users, total number of transactions, and total spends to both merchant and ticker. Data are provided daily, weekly, monthly, and quarterly.
Aggregated Transaction Data		
Electronic Payment Data	Data brokers	A digital payment, sometimes called an *electronic payment*, is the transfer of value from one payment account to another using a digital device, such as a mobile phone, point-of-sale or computer, digital channel communications, etc.

Table E.2—Continued

Category	Example Sources	Definition
Global Transaction Data	Data brokers	A *global transaction* is a mechanism that allows a set of programming tasks, potentially using more than one resource manager and potentially executing on multiple servers, to be treated as one logical unit.
Stock Keeping Unit–Level Transaction Data	Data brokers	Stock keeping unit–level transaction data are similar to credit card transaction data, point-of-sale data, loyalty card data, consumer transaction data, and debit card data.
Retail Data		
Retail Market Data	Data brokers	Information about retail stores, companies, markets, industries, and regions.
Retail Sales Data	Data brokers	Information that powers market research, industry analysis, and retail data analytics for increasing sales, driving growth, and better decisionmaking.
Consumer Review Data	Data brokers	All personal, behavioral, and demographic data that are collected by marketing companies and departments from their customer base.
Consumer Spending Data	Data brokers	*Consumer spending*, or *personal consumption expenditures*, is the value of the goods and services purchased by or on behalf of U.S. residents. At the national level, the Bureau of Economic Analysis publishes annual, quarterly, and monthly estimates of consumer spending.
Brand Data		
Brand Sentiment Data	Data brokers	Measures of the feelings and opinions that people have toward a specific brand. Besides tracking the number of brand mentions on social networks, online reviews, and customer feedback, it also provides context about the tone of the comments and conversations among target audiences.
Brand Affinity Data	Data brokers	*Brand affinity* describes consumers who believe a particular brand shares values in common with them.

Table E.2—Continued

Category	Example Sources	Definition
Industry Data		
Insurance Data	Data brokers	Insurance data to create a picture of who you are and the likelihood that something might happen.
Telecommunications Data	Data brokers	*Telecommunications data* involving the exchange of information over significant distances by electronic means; refers to all types of voice, data, and video transmission
Agricultural Data	U.S. Department of Agriculture, data brokers	Information related to farming, including information on growing crops, rearing animals, managing land, and monitoring weather patterns
National Accounts Data		
Macro Labor Data	IMF, federal government	Unemployment rates, workforce participation, and similar metrics
Macro Production Data	IMF, federal government	Data derived from microdata by statistics on groups or aggregates, such as counts, means, or frequencies
Gross Domestic Product/Gross National Product	IMF, federal government	*Gross domestic product* is the standard measure of the value added created through the production of goods and services in a country during a certain period. *Gross national product* takes into account the manufacturing of tangible goods, such as vehicles, agricultural products, machinery, etc., as well as the provision of such services as health care, business consultancy, and education within a national boundary.

NOTE: EPA = Environmental Protection Agency; FAA = Federal Aviation Administration; IMF = International Monetary Fund; IP = Internet Protocol; NGA = National Geospatial-Intelligence Agency.

Abbreviations

AI	artificial intelligence
ARCYBER	U.S. Army Cyber Command
BDE	brigade
BEA	Bureau of Economic Affairs
CA	civil affairs
COTS	commercial off-the-shelf
DMV	Department of Motor Vehicles
DoD	U.S. Department of Defense
DoDD	Department of Defense Directive
EIS	Enterprise Information Systems
GIS	geographic information systems
GOTS	government off-the-shelf
IE	information environment
IRC	information-related capability
ISIS	Islamic State of Iraq and Syria
IT	information technology
JMWC	Joint Military Information Support Operations WebOps Center
LOE	line of effort
MISO	military information support operations
ML	machine learning
MP	military police
MSR	main supply route
NASA	National Aeronautics and Space Administration
NLP	natural language processing
NOAA	National Oceanic and Atmospheric Administration
OCPA	Office of the Chief of Public Affairs
OIE	operations in the information environment
PA	public affairs
PAI	publicly available information
PAO	public affairs office
PARDIE	Partnership for Analytic Research and Development in the Information Environment
PEO	Program Executive Office
PSYOPS	psychological operations

PWK	Atropia Workers Party
REMVE	racially and ethnically motivated violent extremist
ROI	return on investment
SM	social media
SME	subject-matter expert
SOF	Special Operations Forces
USGS	United States Geological Survey

References

Army Technical Publication 3-13.1, *The Conduct of Information Operations*, Department of the Army, October 2018.

ATP—*See* Army Technical Publication.

Cappa, Francesco, Raffaele Oriani, Enzo Peruffo, and Ian McCarthy, "Big Data for Creating and Capturing Value in the Digitalized Environment: Unpacking the Effects of Volume, Variety, and Veracity on Firm Performance," *Journal of Product Innovation Management*, Vol. 38, No. 1, January 2021.

Chawk, Francis K., "Marine Corps Information Operations Center," *Marine Corps Gazette*, April 2020.

Cheng, Brian, Scott Fisher, and Jason C. Morgan, "Find It, Vet It, Share It: The U.S. Government's Open-Source Intelligence Problem and How to Fix It," Modern War Institute at West Point, March 24, 2023.

Department of Defense Directive 3115.18, *DoD Access to and Use of Publicly Available Information (PAI)*, June 11, 2019, incorporating change 1, August 20, 2020.

Greer, Benjamin, and Eric Wallace, "PARDIE OIE Technology Development Roadmap," Joint Information Operations Warfare Center, June 17, 2020.

Ishwarappa and J. Anuradha, "A Brief Introduction on Big Data 5Vs Characteristics and Hadoop Technology," *Procedia Computer Science*, Vol. 48, 2015.

Smith, Maggie, and Nick Starck, "Open-Source Data Is Everywhere—Except the Army's Concept of Information Advantage," Modern War Institute at West Point, May 24, 2022.

Susha, Iryna, Marijn Janssen, and Stefaan Verhulst, "Data Collaboratives as a New Frontier of Cross-Sector Partnerships in the Age of Open Data: Taxonomy Development," *Proceedings of the 50th Hawaii International Conference on System Sciences*, January 2017.

U.S. Department of Defense, *DoD Dictionary of Military and Associated Terms*, November 2021.